LIVES OF THE BRITISH SAINTS

Inscribed stone known as St David's Staff, Llandewi Brefi Church.

HERMIT SAINT.
From a Drawing by A. Welby Pugin.

LIVES OF THE BRITISH SAINTS

By
S. Baring-Gould
and
John Fisher,
and edited by
Derek Bryce.

ISBN 0947992 37 5

Published by Llanerch Enterprises.

BRITAIN
IN 580.
PICTS
STRATH CLYDE
BERNICIANS
CUMBRIANS
ELMET
DEIRANS
MID ANGLES
MERCIA
GWYNEDD
NORTH WELSH
POWIS
DYFED
GWENT
EAST ANGLES
EAST SAXONS
Bedford 571
Gloucester 577
Deorham 577
WEST SAXONS
Bath 577
Old Sarum 552
JUTES
KENT
Crayford 457
Aylesford 455
STH SAXONS
Portsmouth 501
WEST WELSH

Contents.

Editor's preface.

After about two centuries of materialism since the beginnings of the industrial revolution, it is not easy to appreciate the spiritual qualities of those who made the age of saints, in the fifth and sixth centuries, a period officially described in our times as a dark age. That the people of those times experienced a strong sense of a spiritual presence is witnessed by the many who gave up their family, home, and possessions for the monastic life; not only refugees from the foreign invaders, but many nobles who still had their patrimony.

In reading the lives of these old Celtic saints, it is easy to see their faults, which can be described at length, whereas their holiness, which made them attractive to their disciples, is often described in only a sentence or two, and is really something that can but inadequately be explained in words. It is therefore important to remember that they were saints in spite of, and not because of their short-comings.

In producing an edited, abridged text of Baring-Gould and Fisher's four-volume work, I have aimed at making an interesting book containing some of the more important saints. I apologise to readers who may find that I have missed out some saint, or incident in the life of a saint, which they think important.

Most of the 'lives' of the saints were written, or re-written during the Norman period by monks who were not so much interested in history as promoting the cult of their saint. Therefore, they embellished their texts with miracles, many of which can be recognized as borrowed from lives of other saints. Baring-Gould and Fisher pointed out, quite rightly, that subtracting these miracles does not take one back to an original sixth-century 'life,' for many of the miracles were not simply added, but made by modifying and exaggerating incidents in the original 'lives.' The fact that many miracles were added later, does not mean that there was nothing extra-ordinary or remarkable about these saints, and Baring-Gould and Fisher perhaps went too far to the other extreme in providing rational explanations for almost every unusual incident. In this selection, I have tried to avoid both extremes. I have also taken note of Doble's 'Lives of the Welsh Saints' edited by D Simon Evans, acknowledging comments from it in the text. I have also replaced a suggestion made by Baring-Gould and Fisher that there was an early Saxon occupation of the old Roman fort near Brecon, by an Irish Goidelic occupation, which I think better fits the facts.

Finally, I wish to thank Father Stephen Maxfield for pointing out that Baring-Gould and Fisher set out pedigrees for the saints, without allowing for the use of the term father for a spiritual instructor, as well as in the usual temporal sense. I have added a note about this in the introduction, and elsewhere in the text. This point helps to clear up problems where a saint is given different fathers by different texts; also where one text gives a name as a father, and another the same name as a brother, cousin, etc. Errors arising from a failure to recognize this point can also affect estimated chronologies.

Derek Bryce, Wales, 1990.

Introduction: Celtic Saints.

In Roman Britain there were probably bishops in the principal towns, as London, Lincoln, York and Caerleon, and the Church was organized in the same manner as in Gaul, each bishop having his see, loosely delimited. The Christianity that entered Britain was almost certainly through the soldiery and the Romano-Gallic merchants and settlers in the towns. It spread also into the country, but it is impossible to say to what extent the native British were converted.

But when the Antonine Wall in the North was breached, and there was a rush made south by refugees to Wales, and when others came flying before the swords of the Saxons and Angles, the whole ecclesiastical framework went to pieces. There were no more sees. Bishops were among those who escaped into Wales or crossed the seas to Armorica and Spanish Gallicia, but they had no longer any territorial jurisdiction. In the desolation and confusion of the times, this was inevitable.

As the Celtic Church in Wales began to recover from the shock, it gravitated about new centres, monastic institutions, of which the heads might or might not be bishops. It was so in Ireland after Patrick's time, where no such thing as a territorial organization was attempted till centuries later; there monasteries were attached to tribes and ministered to their religious requirements. Bishops were retained by the abbots, but they had no jurisdiction, they were subject to abbot or abbess, and were retained for the purpose of conferring orders, and for that alone. It began in this way in Brittany, but there the close influence of the Gallo-French Church, and the insistence of the Frank kings, rapidly brought the Celtic Church there into line. Such a tribal organization was in conformity with Celtic ideas, and followed on that which existed in Pagan times. Then there had been the Secular Tribe with its chief at its head, and alongside of it what may be called the Ecclesiastical Tribe, composed of Bards and Druids.

With the acceptance of Christianity, the saints simply occupied the shells left vacant by the Druids. Among the Celts all authority was gathered into the hands of hereditary chiefs. Of these there were two kinds, the military and the ecclesiastical chief, each occupying separate lands; but the members of the ecclestistical tribe were bound to render military service to the secular chief; and the ecclesiastical chief on his side was required to provide for the needs of the secular tribe by educating the young of both sexes, and by performing religious ceremonies. Every tenth child, tenth pig, calf, foal, went to the saint, and the tribe was thus recruited. In certain cases an even more liberal grant was made to the Church, as in Leinster, where, as the 'Colloquy of the Ancients' informs us, "the province dedicated to the saint a third of their children, and a third of their wealth."

There was an economic reason which compelled the Celts to establish great congregations of celibates. Neither in Ireland nor in Wales was the land sufficiently fertile, and the cultivable land sufficiently extensive to maintain the growing population. The only alternatives to compulsory celibacy were war and migration. And we must remember that multitudes of refugees were pressing into Wales from North and East, far more than that mountainous land could sustain.

A story is told in 'Annals of the Four Masters' (O'Donovan, 1851) that shows how serious the problem was even with the aid of the compulsory celibacy of the monasteries. In 657 the population in Ireland had so increased, that the arable land proved insufficient; accordingly an assembly of clergy and laity was summoned by Diarmidh and Blaithmac, Kings of Ireland, to take counsel. It was decided that the amount of land held by any one person should be restricted from the usual allowance of nine ridges of plough land, nine of bog, nine of pasture, and nine of forest; and further the elders of the assembly directed that prayers should be offered to the Almighty to send a pestilence "to reduce the number of the lower class, that the rest might live in comfort." St. Fechin of Fore, on being consulted, approved of this extraordinary petition, and the prayer was answered by the sending of the Yellow Plague; but the vengeance of God caused the pestilence to fall on the nobles and clergy, of whom multitudes, including the kings and Fechin of Fore himself, were carried off.

The duties of the saint were to instruct the young of the tribe, to provide for the religious services required, and to curse the enemies of the Secular Tribe. The institution of schools for the young was certainly much older than Christianity in Britain and Ireland. We know from classical authorities, as well as from Irish writers of the heroic legends, that the Druids formed communities, that these were presided over by an Arch-Druid, that in them were educated the sons of the kings and nobles, and that the heads of these schools had lands for their support. By no other way can we explain the marvellous expansion of the educational establishments which took place after Ireland became Christian, than on the supposition that the saints entered in upon an institution already existing, and brought into it a new life.

St. Kentigern at Llanelwy had 965 monks. At Bangor Iscoed, according to Bede, there were seven choirs, numbering 300 in each. St. Cuana had 1746 scholars under him.

Some of these great schools or monasteries contained females as well as males. St. Brigid at Kildare ruled such a double house of monks as well as nuns. As many of the pupils tarried on to prepare for an ecclesiastical life, these young people were thrown together a good deal, and the results were not always satisfactory. Accordingly one or other of the saints induced a sister or a mother to establish a girl's school, subject to his supervision, yet at a distance from the college of youths, sufficient to prevent the recurrence of scandal.

The people went to the monastery to receive communion, especially at Easter. The churches were small, usually of wattle and daub, and could not hold large congregations, so crosses were erected in various places where a saint would preach and probably also minister the sacrament.

The office of cursing originally formed part of the duties of the Druid. He was a functionary called in likewise at the conclusion of contracts. When two individuals entered into a compact, the Druid was present to utter imprecations on him who should break the agreement. Beside the Druid there was the poet who would guarantee to compose a lampoon against one who should break the contract. This was part and parcel of the legal process. In Ireland, when Sts. Patric, Carentoc, and the rest of the Commission revised the laws, the least possible interference was made with existing social and legal systems.

As the Druid ceased to be esteemed, the saint gradually took over his functions. He had thrust on him the duties formerly discharged by the Druid. From being professional curser of the tribal foes, it was but natural that the saint should take on him to curse those who interfered with the priviliges of the monastery, or even gave him personal offence.

Some related customs survived until the nineteenth century:

In Wales the Holy Well of St. Elian was employed for invoking a curse on offenders. In Brittany, those you had been wronged appealed to St. Yves to punish the wrong doer; and once the right had been accomplished, it was said that it could not be stopped.

We must not be too shocked at this cursing as practised by the Celtic saints. It was a legal right accorded them, hedged about with certain restrictions. It was a means provided by law and custom to enable the weak, who could not redress their wrongs by force of arms, to protect themselves against the mighty, and to recover goods taken from them by force. A man who thought he had been wronged, and could not forcibly put things right according to the law, went to a Druid in Pagan times, to a saint in Christian days, and asked him to "ill-wish" the wrong-doer, just as now he goes to a layer and solicits a summons.

In Wales, as in Ireland, the law could be ascertained, and the amount of fine decreed, but the aggrieved was left to his own devices to obtain the redress. The court did nothing to enforce its judgements. A man who could not use force of arms was left with two courses: either he might get a saint to curse the debtor, or else, he might take the matter into his own hands by "fasting against" the offender.

The process was this. He made formal demand for what was due to him. If this were refused, he seated himself at the door of the debtor and abstained from food and drink. The debtor could resist by fasting also.

Many Celtic saints used fasting as a weapon, and everything conduced to engage the first missionaries in a contest of ascetic emulation with the medicine men of Paganism. They strove to outstrip them, for if they fell short of the extremes practised by the latter, they could not hope to gain the ear of the princes and impress the common people. It is said of St. Kevin, for example, that he remained seven years without sleep, and that he held up one arm till it became rigid. St. Erc is said to have spent the day immersed in a river. St. Ita to have had only earth for her bed.

Despite all the foregoing, it is important not to forget that these old Celtic saints had also the holiness or sanctity that goes with their title.

The fifth and sixth centuries mark the age of saints of the Celtic Church. The saints of Wales belong to eight great families:

1. That of Maxen Wledig, or Maximus, 383-338, He is held to have married a daughter of Eudaf, a petty prince in Arfon, and Aurelius Ambrosius probably claimed descent from Maximus. From the same stock came Rhydderch Hael, king of Strathclyde/Cumbria; also Ynyr Gwent, prince of Gwent, who lived at Caerwent. This family would seem to have represented Romano-British civilisation.

2. That of Cunedda, which came from the North, from the defence of the Wall. This family is said to have expelled the Irish Goidels from Gwynedd, Ceredigion, and Môn (Anglesey). The royal line of Gwynedd came from this family; it only came to an end with the last Llewelyn. This is one of the three saintly families or tribes of Wales, and

from it came Saints Dewi and Teilo.

3. That of Cadell Deyrnllwg who became prince of Powys in the fifth century. This family produced several saints, including Tyssilio of Meifod, Pedrog and Catwg.

4. That of Brychan, king of Brycheinog. This was an Irish family which came to be regarded as one of the three holy families of Wales; it produced an incredible number of Saints who are found not only in their native district, but also in North-east and East Cornwall.

5. That of Caw in North Britain, the third saintly family. Caw, however, was son of Geraint ab Erbin, prince of Dumnonia. Owing to the inroads of the Picts, the family of Caw were obliged to flee to Gwynedd where they were well received by Cadwallon Lawhir, and Maelgwn, his son, who gave them lands, mainly in Anglesey, apparently with the proviso that they should enter religion, so as not to form any small principalities which might be politically damaging to the interests of the crown of Gwynedd. To this family belonged Gildas, the famous abbot of Ruys.

6. That of Coel Godebog. According to Skene, he was king in North Britain, and his name is preserved in Kyle. He was ancestor of an important family which includes Urien Rheged, Llwyarch Hen, and Saints Pabo, Dunawd, and Deiniol of Bangor.

7. That of Csytennin Gorneu, a family derived from a usurper of the Roman purple, Constantine the Tyrant. This family would seem to have provided Dumnonia (Devon and Cornwall) with its princes, who were called either Constantine or Geraint. St Cybi came from this family; the notorius Constantine himself was eventually converted. The family of Caw (5, above) is descended from this stock.

St. Patrick.
Stained glass, St. Neot, Cornwall.

8. That of Emyr Llydaw from Armorica. All that we know about Emyr is that, on account of an usurpation of one of his sons, the others had to flee to South Wales where they were received by Meurig, king of Morganwg, who gave to several of them his daughters in marriage. The Bretons claim that the eldest son, who sent the family flying, was Llywel or Hoel "the Great." From Emyr proceeded such great men as Sts. Samson and Padarn, and, by a daughter, Saints Cadfan and Winwaloe.

Although the most obvious features which distinguished the Celtic Church from the Roman were the shape of the monk's tonsure and the method of calculating the date of Easter, there must also have been differences associated with tribalism and the way in which Christianity had replaced the Druidic Tradition. A consequence of tribalism in the Celtic lands was that the position of Abbot became hereditary, and a candidate had to prove his pedigree before having any chance of the position, a situation which gave rise to complaints of injustice centuries later. The pedigrees and dates given in this work should be taken only as tentative; mistakes can be made in the early Christian period by taking a spiritual father as a temporal one, which also affects the chronology.

There are reasons for thinking that the religious revival in post-Roman Wales is not so much derived from the original Romano-British Christianity, as from new monastic ideals coming from abroad, by sea. The age of saints saw the Celtic Church in Wales sending a stream of missionaries to Ireland to complete the conversion begun by Patrick, himself a child of somewhere in the west of Britain. It was from Ireland that Columba went to Iona, to become the evangelist of the Picts. From Llanelwy went forth Kentigern with

St. Austell.
Statue on Tower, St. Austell.

665 monks and clerics to restore Christianity in Strathclyde/Cumbria, from the Clyde to the Dee. It was from Iona that Northumbria received its Christianity; also Mercia, the East Saxons and Angles. To them also was due the conversion of much of Armorican Brittany, and some of the Welsh saints, on route for Armorica, established foundations in Cornwall; St. Austell, for example. St. Augustine of Canterbury was not, therefore, the main source from whom Christianity sprang in Britain. He was the Apostle of Kent; but Kent is only one corner of the island of Britain; it has so often been forgotten how much was wrought by the Celtic Church, even for the Teutonic invaders, far more than was achieved by Augustine.

Of some of the Welsh saints we know only their names, from the original dedications of churches, some of which were re-dedicated in Norman times to saints from the Roman calendar. Of others, we have written 'lives,' sometimes complete, sometimes fragmentary. Such written lives are almost all manuscript copies made at a much later date than the original, some in Latin, some in Welsh. The copies are frequently embellished to suit the intentions of the times. Many copies made in Norman times were greatly embellished by the addition of spurious miracles, sometimes, as in the case of the Book of Llandaff, to suit the claims of the see to territories claimed by other bishoprics. It is therefore important to remember that the mediaeval copyists were seldom motivated in their work from a sense of history.

Tomb of Pabo Post Prydain,
Llanbabo, Anglesey.

St. Asaph.

St Asaph or Asa lived during the latter part of the sixth and the beginning of the seventh century. There was a 'life' of him written in the Red Book of St. Asaph, the original of which has since been lost. Only a fragment of this 'life' has survived in an imperfect transcript. It makes reference to "the sweetness of his conversation, the symmetry, vigour, and elegance of his body, the virtues and sanctity of his heart, and the manifestation of his miracles."

Most of what we know about St. Asaph comes from the Life of St. Kentigern, written about 1180 by Jocelin, a monk of Furness. Jocelin says that St. Asaph was "distinguished by birth" and we find that his grandfather was St. Pabo Post Prydyn or Prydain, "the Pillar of North Britain, or Britain." Pabo himself was descended in the fourth degree from Coel Hen, "Old King Cole." Pabo began life in the North where he distinguished himself as a brave warrior. But eventually he lost his territory and went to seek refuge in Wales, where he was given lands by Cyngen ab Cadell, prince of Powys. Later he took up the religious life and was accounted a saint of the British Church. St. Asaph was also a nephew of St. Dunawd and a cousin of St. Deiniol, founder and first bishop of Bangor.

St. Asaph was very probably a native of the cantref of Tegeingl in Flintshire. When still a boy he was placed under St. Kentigern, the exiled bishop of the Strathclyde Britons, at his monastery on the Elwy, founded about 560. This foundation had become so famous that some 965 monks were said there to follow Kentigern's monastic rule.

Jocelin tells us that among the brotherhood was "one Asaph by name, distinguished by birth and presence, shining in virtues and miracles from the flower of his earliest youth. He sought to follow the life and teaching of his master, as may be learnt from reading a little book on his life, from which I have thought fit to insert in this work one miracle, because the perfection of the disciple is the glory of the master. For on one occasion, in the time of winter, when the frost had contracted and congealed everything, St. Kentigern, having according to his custom recited the Psalter naked in the coldest water, and having after putting on his clothes gone out in public, he began to be greatly oppressed by the intensity of the cold, and in a measure to become entirely rigid... The holy father therefore ordered the boy Asaph to bring fire to him, at which he might warm himself. The boy ran to the oven and begged that coals night be given to him. And when he had nothing in which to carry the burning coals, the servant said to him either in joke or seriously: 'if you wish to take the coals, hold out your dress, for I have nothing to hand in which you may carry them.' The holy boy, fervent in faith, and trusting in the sanctity of the master, without hesitating, held out his dress, and received the live coals into his lap, and carrying them to the old man cast them from his bosom without there being any sign of burning on his dress. This astonished all who were present. A friendly dispute arose between the father and this holy disciple concerning this sign, for the one seemed to maintain his ground by assertions to which the other objected. The bishop ascribed the working of the sign to the innocence and obedience of the holy boy; the boy asserted that it was done on account of the merits and sanctity of the bishop, obeying whose command and trusting in whose whose holiness he had ventured to attempt it."

St. Asaph.
From 15th. cent. glass,
Llandyrnog Church, Denbighshire.

As a result of the Battle of Arderydd fought in 573, Rhydderch Hael established himself as King of Strathclyde/Cumbria, and St. Kentigern's exile in Wales was ended. King Rhydderch recalled him to the North, where he eventually established the seat of his bishopric in Glasgow, but before leaving Llanelwy he addressed the brotherhood, and, "with the unanimous consent of all, appointed St. Asaph to the government of the monastery, and by petition of the people, and by the canonical election of the clergy, sucessor to his bishopric... When the sermon was ended he enthroned St. Asaph in the cathedral seat, and again blessing and bidding them all farewell, he went forth by the north door of the church, because he was going forth to combat a northern enemy. When he had gone out, that door was closed, and all who saw or heard of his going out or departure bewailed his absence with great lamentations. Hence the custom grew up in that church that that door should not be opened except once a year, on the festival of St. Asaph, that is, on the Kalends of May, for two reasons. First, in deference to the sanctity of him who had gone forth; secondly, because thereby was indicated the great grief of those who had bewailed his departure. Therefore, on the day of St. Asaph that door is opened, because when he succeeded the blessed Kentigern in the government their mourning was turned into joy. From that monastery a great part of the bretheren, to the number of 665, being in no wise able or willing, so long as he lived, to live without him, went with him. Only 300 remained with St. Asaph."

Llanelwy has always been the Welsh name of St. Kentigern's foundation; it was given the name of St. Asaph by the English early in the twelfth century.

St. Beuno.

Most of what we know of St. Beuno comes from a short life written in Welsh, several manuscript copies of which have survived; the oldest one was made in 1346 at Llanddewi Brefi in Cardiganshire.

St. Beuno is said to have been the son of Bugi, who lived in Powys and who himself also became a saint towards the end of his life.

The young Beuno was sent to Caerwent to be educated by St. Tangusius, in the college founded by Ynyr Gwent. Here he "obtained a knowledge of all the Holy Scriptures; afterwards he learned the service of the Church and its rules, and took orders and became a priest." It is said that Ynyr Gwent himself, in his old age, granted Beuno lands in Ewyas, and that he became his disciple. This is now Llanfeuno, a chapelry under Clodock, near Longtown in Herefordshire. Whilst there, Beuno heard that his father was ill, and he committed his foundation in Ewyas to three of his disciples, and went to Powys, "and his father, after receiving communion, making his confession, and rendering his end perfect, departed this life." Beuno made a foundation there, and planted an acorn by his father's grave. It grew into a mighty tree of which one branch curved down to the ground, and then rose again, "and there was a part of this branch in the soil, as at present; and if an Englishman should pass between this branch and the trunk of the tree, he would immediately die; but should a Welshman go, he would in no way suffer."

Next Beuno was granted land at Berriew near Welshpool in Montgomeryshire; a standing stone called the Maen Beuno marks the spot where he is said to have preached to the people. One day, however, when he was walking by the Severn, he

St. Gwenfrewi, sister of Beuno.
15th. century glass, Llandyrnog Church.

heard the hunting cries of an Englishman from across the river, and he went to his disciples and said: "My sons, put on your clothes and shoes, and let us leave this place, for the nation of the man with the strange language, whose cry I heard beyond the river urging on his hounds, will invade this place, and it will be theirs, and they will hold it as their possession."

Then he commended his foundation at Berriew to a disciple named Rhithwlint, and spent forty days and nights at Meifod with St. Tyssilio, after which Cynan, son of Brochewl of Powys, gave him lands in Meirionethshire, at Gwyddelwern, near Corwen. Gwyddelwern implies the site of an Irish settlement, but the 'life' says that it was so called because Beuno raised an Irishman back to life there. He was probably Llorcan Wyddel, mentioned as one of the six persons said to have been raised by him. Beuno did not stay long on this spot, because of trouble with Cynan's grandsons, the sons of Selyf, who came and demanded food for themselves and their party. Beuno killed a young ox for them, but they complained that he had bewitched the food. When he heard this, he cursed the young men, saying: "What your grandfather gave to God free, do you demand of it tribute and service? May your kin never possess the land, and may you be destroyed out of this kingdom and be likewise deprived of your eternal inheritance." Truly it was a risky thing to interfere with these old Celtic saints! The real facts seem to have been that the young men claimed food and shelter as a right, such as they could demand of any lay householder in the tribe; but this was precisely a claim from which the ecclesiastics considered themselves to be exempt.

As a result of this event Beuno left Powys and went to Flintshire, in the Kingdom of Gwynedd.

St. Beuno.
From the open-air pulpit, Shrewsbury Abbey.

About the year 612, Cadfan, king of Gwynedd died, and Beuno visited his son Cadwallon, making him a present of a gold sceptre that he had been given by Cynan of Powys. In return, Cadwallon gave Beuno a patch of land at Gwredog in Arfon. There the saint built a church, and began to enclose it by an earthen bank. Whilst he was doing this, a woman came with a baby, and asked the saint to bless it. "Presently," he replied, "as soon as this job is finished." But the child's cries disturbed him so much that he asked the woman why her baby was squealing all the time. "He has good reason," replied the mother, "for you are enclosing land that belonged to his father and is properly his." On hearing this, Beuno shouted to his monks: "Leave off this work, and, whilst I baptize this child, make my chariot ready. We will go to the king with this woman and child."

So they went to see Cadwallon in Caersaint (Carnarvon) and Beuno said to him: "Why did you give me the land when it was not yours to give, but belonged to this child? Give me other land, or else return to me the gold sceptre worth sixty cows that I gave to you."

"I will give you nothing else," replied the king; "and as for the sceptre, I have already given it away."

Then Beuno in great wrath, cursed Cadwallon: "I pray to God that you may not long possess the land."

And then he left, but when he had crossed the river Saint, he sat on a stone, and a cousin of Cadwallon caught up with him. His name was Gwyddaint, and "for his own soul and that of Cadwallon" he offered him his own township of Clynnog, "without tribute or service, or any one having any claim on it." Beuno readily accepted, and from then onwards, Clynnog became his main abode. It is beautifully situated on the north coast of Lleŷn, under the mountains of Bwlch Mawr and Gyrn Ddu.

Now it happened that a skilled and handsome young carpenter from Aberffraw was invited to Caerwent, to build a palace there. Whilst he was there, Tigiwg the daughter of Ynyr the king, fell in love with him, and accompanied him on his journey back home. But the carpenter was not particularly amorous, or was ashamed of taking a princess to his native hovel, and on the way back he murdered her, or so the legend says. She was found by Beuno's Shepherds who reported the matter to the saint. He resuscitated her and induced her to lead the religious life. (It is possible that she was simply deserted, rather than killed, by the carpenter). After a while, rumour of what had happened reached Caerwent, and Iddon, her brother, came in search of her. His sister, however, refused to return, either from a preference for the religious life or from fear of having made far to great a fool of herself over the carpenter. Her brother accepted this, but he asked Beuno to go with him to Aberffraw to support his claim for the "horses and gold and silver" which the carpenter had carried off along with his sister. Beuno agreed to this, and off they went to the court of Cadwallon at Aberffraw. As soon as Iddon set eyes on the young carpenter, he drew his sword and would have killed him but for those who were standing nearby holding him back. At first Cadwallon refused to have the goods restored, but Beuno insisted, and the king, perhaps afraid of incurring another curse, gave way; he also gave Beuno the palace called Aelwyd Feuno. Beuno returned to Clynnog, well content, and remained there the rest of his days.

A story that Iddon cut off the carpenter's head,

and that Beuno replaced it, is no doubt a later mediaeval embellishment.

St. Beuno was buried in a chapel on the south-west side of the church. It is said to have been destroyed by those searching for his relics. His holy well, Ffynon Feuno, is about 200 yards from the church. In former days, rickety and epileptic children, as well as impotent folk generally, were dipped in it, and then carried to the chapel and put to lie overnight on the saint's tombstone. If they slept, they would be cured.

A custom that survived until the early nineteenth century was one of making offerings of calves and lambs which happened to be born with a slit in the ear, popularly called Beuno's Mark. These "sacred beasts" were brought to church on Trinity Sunday, and the church-wardens who sold them put the proceeds into Cyff Beuno (Beuno's chest). Into the chest also went the offerings of persons who came from distant parts of the country, even down to the early nineteenth century, to propitiate the saint on behalf of their cattle when afflicted with some disorder. When the chest was opened in December, 1688, it contained £15.8.3d. The money was used for church repairs and the relief of the poor.

St. Beuno's chest at Clynnog.

Head of St. Beuno.
From window at Penmorfa, Carnarvon.

St. Beuno's Well, Clynnog.

St. Brychan, King.

LIttle is known about this mysterious king. A brief Latin tract provides us with a legend of his birth and upbringing:

There was a king Tewdrig of Garthmadryn, who came to live near Llanfaes in the neighbourhood of Brecon. Tewdrig had a daughter, Marchell, to whom he said: "The sharpness of the cold weather greatly affects you, and it will be well to procure for you a fur garment. I will send you to Ireland, with three hundred men, to Anlach, son of King Coronac, who will marry you." Then Marchell set forth with her retinue and on the first night one hundred of the men died of cold. On the second night, at Methrum, probably Meidrum in Carmarthenshire, a second hundred died. The third night was spent at Porthmawr, by St. David's Head, which must have been a warmer place, for she sailed from there with the remaining hundred men, to Ireland. When she reached the court of Anlach, he received her dancing with joy, and made her his wife. Marchell gave birth to a son whom they first called Brachan, later Brychan. And Anlach returned with Queen Marchell and the boy Brychan to Wales. And the boy was sent to be fostered by one Drichan. And in his seventh year Drichan said to Brychan: "Bring my lance to me." Drichan later became blind, and whilst he lay awake, a boar came from the wood and stood by the banks of the river Ysçir; and there was a stag behind it in the river, and also a fish beneath the stag, all of which was taken a portending that Brychan should be happy in abundance and wealth. Likewise there was a beech tree by the same river, in which bees made honey, and Drichan said to his pupil Brychan: "Lo, I give you this tree full of bees and honey, and also of gold

St. Marchell, mother of Brychan.
15th. century glass, Llandyrnog Church.

St. Brychan.
From stained glass window, St. Neot, Cornwall.

and silver; and may the grace of God, and His love, abide with you always, here and hereafter."

After that, Anlach gave Brychan as hostage to the king of Powys; and Brychan came to violate the king's daughter, and she became pregnant, giving birth to a son whom they called Cynog.

The legend goes on to give the names of the wives and sons and daughters of Brychan, for he is famous as the founder-father of one of the three saintly tribes of Wales. The large numbers of sons and daughters attributed to him by various traditional sources should be taken as including also some of his grandchildren. Our illustration of St. Brychan from a stained glass window at St. Neot, Cornwall, shows him with many children.

According to legend, the grave of Anlach, father of Brychan, is before the door of Llanspyddid Church. In the churchyard there, there is a stone called the "Cross of Brychan Brycheinog". Llanspyddid is dedicated to St. Cadoc, a grandson of Brychan. Llanhamlach may contain the name of Anlach, and an early sculptured stone there shows saints with arms raised in the ancient attitude of prayer.

Passing from legend to history, it is possible that Anlach was leader of an invading band of Irish Goidels who settled in Wales, and that by marrying the daughter of King Tewdrig he won the good will of the inhabitants, and that his tribe remained, intermixed with the Welsh. Garthmadryn was replaced by a new name, Brycheinog, derived from that of its new ruler; it included much of Brecknockshire. It is very likely that Anlach settled in what was left of the walled city of Bannium, now known as Y Gaer, near Brecon in the Usk valley.

Cross of Brychan Brycheinog, Llanspyddid.

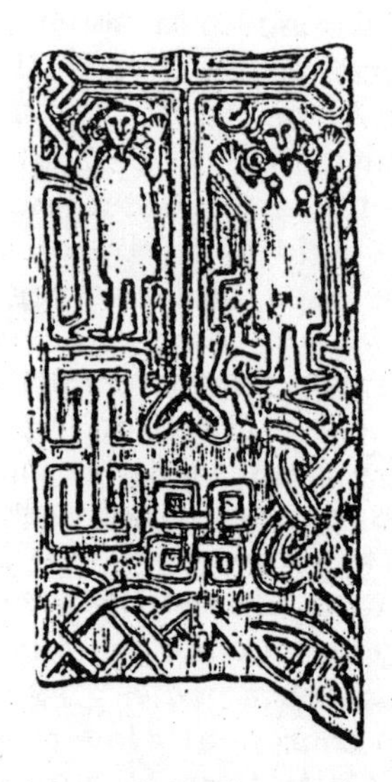

Stone showing saints in ancient attitude of prayer, Llanhamlach.

St. Brynach.

Brynach Wyddel, or "the Irishman," was married to Corth or Cymorth, one of the daughters of Brychan. He was a priest, and spiritual instructor to the king and his family. Not only was he priest, but also abbot.

A Latin life of him, of the twelfth century, seems to have been based on Welsh ballads.

For a while he was in Armorica, and when he desired to come to Wales he put a stone on the water and mounted it, and was wafted over to Milford Haven. There the daughter of the prince became enamoured of him, but as he resisted her advances, she sent men to murder him, and one stabbed him with a lance. Thereupon a swarm of winged ants fell upon the man, and so stung him that he suffered greatly, and died. The saint then bathed his wound in a spring, ever after called Ffynnon Goch or the Red Well.

Eventually, he went to the river Caman in Pembrokeshire, where an angel had informed him that a site for a monastery would be pointed out to him by a wild white boar and her litter. Here he lit a fire, and this was regarded as the assertion of a right to the place. The lord of the district seeing the smoke came hastily to know who had dared to light a fire; but he was a good man and he gave land to St. Brynach and committed his sons to him for their education. The saint now built a church at the foot of Carn Ingli, above Nevern. There is a story that St. David visited Brynach while on his way to Brevi, and that Brynach obtained a gift of a stone cross from him. The church at Nevern has a very fine ornamented Celtic cross, but of a later date than St. Brynach.

St. Cadoc or Catwg, Abbot, Bishop.

There is a life of this saint written by Lifris or Leofric who was the son of Bishop Herwald (1056-1104). This is the most important of all the lives of Welsh saints written in Wales. There is also a life written in Brittany, by Albert the Great.

Gwynllyw, king of Gwynllywg, had married Gwladys, probably the grand-daughter of Brychan, and had carried her off. Cadoc was their son. Gwynllyw who was a lawless tyrant, had sent his robber bands into Gwent, beyond the Usk, and had carried off the cow of an Irish hermit, whose name was Tathan. The hermit went to the king to implore him to return his cow, but Gwynllyw retained him to baptize his child, and it was given the name of Cathmail. Although he was given this name, he is always known as Cadoc or Catwg.

Later on, the boy was entrusted to the hermit to be educated at Caerwent, where he had a college that had been founded by Ynyr, king of that portion of Gwent. "And he, willingly receiving him, diligently instructed him for twelve years."

The story is told of Cadoc, as of so many other Celtic saints, that he brought live coals to his master in the lap of his habit; and that the place where the coals were concealed was well known till the first half of the eleventh century, and then forgotten. In this case there may be some basis of fact. Cadoc may have discovered a seam of coal, not in Gwent, but in Morganwg, and this the natives continued to use until the irruption of the Normans when the place was abandoned and forgotten.

Cathmail or Cadoc returned to his father, but having resolved on a spiritual life, he deserted his father's home and lands, and went into Morganwg, to the lands of his uncle Paul or Pol of Penychen.

St. Gwynllyw, father of Cadoc.
From statue at St. Woolo's.

There he wandered about alone in a marshy district, and coming suddenly on a herd of swine belonging to Paul, scared and scattered them. The swineherd, incensed at this, raised his spear, and would have transfixed him, had not Cadoc told him his name and relationship to his master.

When Paul learned that his nephew was wandering homeless on his territory, he sent for him and offered him some land on which to settle. Cadoc gladly accepted the marshy valley where he had met the swineherd, and his uncle made it over to him.

In one part of the marsh, where there was higher ground, a swan had nested, and there also an old grey boar had its lair. As Cadoc was looking about for a suitable spot on which to erect his wattled cell, he disturbed the swan and the boar. The former flew away, but the boar retired reluctantly, and turned three times to look at the man who had invaded its retreat. Cadoc staked out the ground, marking the spots where the boar had halted, and resolved to plant his monastery there, and build his church, refectory, and dormitory at the points where the beast had turned to watch him. He was soon joined by other young men, probably some of his fellow students who had no liking for the rowdy career of a man of war; and this was the beginning of the famous monastery of Llancarfan.

"Then the holy man undertook to throw up a large mound of earth, and to make therein a very beautiful cemetery, to be dedicated to the honour of God; in which the bodies of the faithful might be buried around the temple. The mound being completed, and the cemetery finished in it, he made four large paths over rising grounds about his cell." After that his buildings of wood were completed, and he looked for another site that would serve as a place of refuge in the event of political incursions or civil war, and chose a hill-top, now Llanfeithin, and there also he threw up a mound that was circular, and on it erected a castle, called Castell Cadog.

The biographer goes on to relate how, "after a long space of time," Cadoc left his monastery and went to Ireland. There he studied for three years, probably under Carthagh, at Saighir.

He returned from Ireland with a large company of Irish and British clergy, including Finnian. Instead of going straight back to Llancarfan, as we might have expected, he placed himself under a celebrated rhetorician, Bachan, in Brecknock. Bachan "had come from Italy" and Cadoc "much desired to be taught Latin after the method of the Romans."

Llanspyddid was over against the Romano-British town, now Y Gaer, and which may have been called by the Romans Bannium. At the entrance to the church of Llanspyddid lay Anlach, the father of Brychan, and grandfather or great-grandfather of Cadoc.

Whilst Cadoc studied at Llanspyddid, famine raged in the land, and the master and his pupils were in dire straits for food. However, Cadoc observed a mouse carrying a grain of wheat. He succeeded in catching it, and borrowing a thread from a widow, tied it to the mouse's foot and let it run; whereupon it darted into a hole. Cadoc dug on the spot, and discovered an underground chamber stored with grain. Such secret granaries were by no means uncommon, and are found in many ancient Welsh and Scottish forts. Or it may have been that one of the hypocausts that have been discovered at Y Gaer had been used as a storehouse for grain. On this supply the master and his pupils were able to live for some time.

Brychan now gave the land at Llanspyddid to his grandson Cadoc, who appointed his teacher Bachan to be abbot there, and departed. It is possible that to this period belongs the foundation of Llangadog Fawr in Carmarthenshire, also in Brychan territory.

It is possibly whilst Cadoc was at Llangadog that he was annoyed by Sawyl Benuchel, a ruffian who was established nearby (and who may have become converted in his old age, for there is a Llansawel there). This Sawyl Benuchel should not be confounded with the brother of Dunawd, who had the same name.

A story goes that one day Sawyl and his party broke into St. Cadoc's monastery and carried off meat and drink. Cadoc was absent at the time, but on his return he was informed that they were a little distance away, eating and drinking.

After they had gorged themselves with meat and ale, Sawyl and his rogues lay down to sleep. Cadoc seized the opportunity to inflict on them a stinging insult. He set his monks to shave half the heads of the drunken men, and then with the razors to slash off the ears and lips of the horses.

When the barbers had done their work, Cadoc and fifty of his monks assumed their ecclesiastical dress, and marched in procession to meet, and if at all possible, mitigate the resentment of the freebooter.

The story says that the earth opened and swallowed up Sawyl and his men. Perhaps some of them perished in a bog afterwards? In any case, they would probably have been ashamed to have been seen around those parts again.

After this, Cadoc sung Te Deum, and blessed the men who had made his adversaries ridiculous.

About this time, Cadoc seems to have returned to his original settlement at Llancarfan, which he found deserted and in ruins. "He beheld the principal monastery destroyed, and the rafters of the roofs and the rubbish of the building scattered over the cemetery; and greiving at the ruin, he earnestly desired to rebuild it." He ordered all his monks, clerics and workmen, to go into the woods and cut timber for the structure.

There is a story that two Irish youths were exempted from this labour, namely Finnian and Macmoil, but Finnian was no doubt older than Cadoc. The steward, cook, and sexton seeing these Irish reading, ordered them to work in the woods. Finnian left his book on the ground where it was not affected by a rain shower, and Cadoc erected an oratory dedicated to him over the spot. This episode may have been included by the biographer in an attempt to explain the existence of a Finnian chapel there; it was more likely erected there by Cadoc simply in honour of his friend.

About this time, Cadoc's father Gwynllyw fell sick and died. Before his death he had been converted by his son. And when he felt himself dying he sent for Cadoc and Bishop Dyfrig. "And they came to the sick person and gave him penance, exhorting and comforting him with salutary doctrine. After this, the bishop pronounced absolution and apostolical benediction."

About this time also, Gildas passed through Penychen, and visited Cadoc. He had with him a bell, to which Cadoc took a fancy, and which he offered to buy; but Gildas refused to part with it, saying he intended it for the Bishop of Rome. Later, however, Gildas gave the bell to Cadoc, saying that the Bishop of Rome had declined it when he heard that so illustrious a man had expressed a desire to possess it. Cadoc seems to have believed this flattery, but has it been added?

It would appear that Gildas visited Llancarfan in 528. Cadoc seized on the occasion to ask Gildas to take charge of his monastery for him, whilst he himself went into Alba (Scotland). To this Gildas consented.

Before Cadoc left for the north, Gildas and David had fallen out over which of them should be head of ecclesiastics in Dyfed. Cadoc avoided being personally involved in this matter, and passed the thankless task to his friend St. Finnian, later Finnian of Clonard. The judgment was in favour of David, and Cadoc now departed for Alba where he built a monastery of stone "near the mountain Bannauc."

The mountain Bannauc seems to be the Cathkin Hills near Carmunnock, and the monastery seems to have been at Cambuslang close by. A curious story attaches to the founding of this monastery in Scotland. Whilst digging the foundations, Cadoc came across some bones, and prayed that it might be revealed to him whose they were. That night a gigantic man appeared to him and told him that they were his earthly remains, and that he was Caw, surnamed Prydyn, and that he had been king beyond the mountain range (i.e. in Strathclyde) but had fallen there in battle. What seems to be the explanation is that at the request of Gildas, Cadoc had sought out the burial mound of his father, Caw of Cwm Cawlwyd, who had been engaged in conflict with the Gwyddyl Ffichti from Ireland, and had lost his territory to them. Then as a token of friendly feeling to Gildas, Cadoc erected his monastery over the tomb of the father of that saint. Caw is similar to Cawr, a giant, which may have given the idea in the legend that Caw was of gigantic proportions.

On the return of Cadoc to Llancarfan, he resumed the rule over his abbey, and Gildas retired to Glastonbury; but these two friends were wont during Lent to retreat to the Steep and Flat Holmes (islands) in the Severn estuary, for prayer and meditation, broken only by visits to one another.

Cadoc's monastery at Llancarfan had grown to one of great importance and wealth. The legend represents his power there as princely. "He daily fed a hundred clergy, and a hundred soldiers, and a hundred workmen, and a hundred poor men, with the same number of widows. This was the number of his household, besides servants in attendance, and esquires, and guests, whose number was uncertain, and a multitude of whom used to visit him frequently. Nor is it strange that he was a rich man and supported many, for he was abbot and prince over the territory (Gwynllywg) of his father from Ffynnon Hen, that is, the Old Well, as far as the mouth of the river Rumney, and he possessed the whole territory from the river Golych as far as the river Dawon, from Pentyrch right on to the valley of Nantcarfan, and from that valley to the river Gurimi, that is, the Lesser Rumney, towards the sea."

About the year 534 Gildas went back to his monastic settlement at Ruys in Armorica. It is possible that Cadoc also went to Brittany "with a few of his monks," about this time. Lifris says that he went there after his father's death. It is, however, possible that Cadoc's visit to Armorica took place at the time of the outbreak of the yellow plague, in 547, when many clerics from South Wales fled to Brittany. Cadoc also made a pilgrimage to Jerusalem and Rome; it is possible in fact that he visited Armorica more than once, stopping off to visit Gildas on the way from, or to Rome, and returning there at a later date.

It was during one of Cadoc's journeys abroad

St. Cadoc.
From statuette at Lampaul-Guimiliau.

that the Synod of Llandewi Brefi was held, perhaps in 545 or 546, before the outbreak of the yellow plague. It could not have been later than 552, for Finnian of Clonard died in that year, and it was he who was deputed to tell Cadoc about it. Cadoc was furious at such a meeting having been held without his being consulted and invited to be present. And his resentment was specially directed against David, for the leading part he had taken in it. In his wrath he proceeded to "fast against" David; he was only induced to desist when it was shown him that his conduct was contrary to principles of Christian charity.

When in Armorica, Cadoc settled an island in the near land-locked sea of Belz, now known as the Ile de S. Cadou. This island is linked to the

Ile de S. Cadou, near Belz.

mainland by a causeway made of massive blocks of granite brought from the neighbouring moors. This is attributed to St. Cadoc. "He erected an elegant church with stones, and afterwards caused to be built by masons a stone bridge skilfully constructed with arched work and having its arches cemented with mortar." Such is the description given by Lifris. Actually, there are no arches, and the blocks of stone were never laid in mortar. In the south transept of the chapel is a structure of granite blocks called St. Cadoc's Bed.

St. Cadoc's Bed.

But to return to Britain, there are a few more stories concerning Cadoc:

One tale is that he converted St. Illtyd, after the latter's hunting companions had been swallowed up by the earth. This story reminds us of the one about Sawyl Benuchel. It seems likely that Illtyd went hunting in the swamp near where St. Cadoc built his monastery. Perhaps his companions lost their lives, and Illtyd himself only just escaped, leading him to think of religion. It is not certain that St. Cadoc was involved.

It is posible that this legend was put forward in order to support the precedence of St. Cadoc's monastery over the rival house founded by St. Illtyd.

Another story tells of one Ligessauc Lawhir

who had killed three of Arthur's knights, and then been given seven years sanctuary by Cadoc. When Arthur eventually found out where this man was, he marched to the banks of the Usk and demanded that the case should be gone into formally. Cadoc got a number of Saints to act on his behalf, including David, Teilo, and Aidan, and the discussion was conducted across the muddy river in shouts. At last it was settled by the judges that Arthur should receive three good oxen for each of his men that had been slain.

Cadoc also became involved in a quarrel with Maelgwn, although he was not to blame. Maelgwn had sent his receivers of tribute into Gwynllywg, and, finding that Cadoc's steward had a pretty daughter, they carried her off. Thereupon the men of the neighbourhood assembled, pursued the ravishers, killed some and wounded others, and recovered the girl. Maelgwn was furious, and marched to the frontiers of Gwynllywg to lay it waste with fire and sword. The inhabitants in alarm sent word to Cadoc, who at once went to Maelgwn and explained to him the affair in its true light, and succeeded in pacifying him.

During the life of Maelgwn, that prince took care not to offend Cadoc, and he laid strict injunctions on his son Rhun, when he was pillaging in South Wales, not to meddle with the possessions of the Abbot of Llancarfan.

However, one day when Rhun was on a plundering foray, and was in his tent playing dice with some eunuchs, some of his men went to a dairy on the possessions of Cadoc, and being thirsty asked for milk. The dairyman refused, and the men, highly incensed, set fire to the barn. The wind carried the smoke to where Rhun was, and he inquired what was burning. When told he sent for Cadoc and apologized for what had been done, assured him it was against his express orders, and to make compensation, gave him his sword, shield and spear.

Rhain, son of Brychan, king of Brycheiniog, "plundered and laid waste" the province of Gwynllywg to the sea. Thereupon the men of Gwynllywg rose in a body, pursued the marauder and defeated him in one battle after another and captured him, but dared not put him to death, because he was of the kin of Cadoc, whose mother was Gwladys, sister of this ruffian. Cadoc, hearing of the straits Rhain was in, went to him, and obtained his liberation.

Cadoc probably went to Ireland in his old age. King Ainmire summoned Gildas to assist in the reviving of religion in Ireland, and he probably extended the invitation to Cadoc and David as all three saints are considered as having given forms of the Mass. Whether David went there, or just sent advice, is not known. This was probably in 564. Cadoc was granted lands on the banks of the Liffey, but he probably did not stay there for long.

Cadoc was now advanced in years, and on his return to Llancarfan he found the management of so large an establishment beyond his strength. He nominated Elli, a favourite disciple, as his successor. He left the bretheren of Llancarfan a Book of the Gospels, and appointed that all trials and settlments of disputes should take place under a hazel tree he had planted. After that, he departed, disappearing into a cloud that conveyed him to Beneventum, which may be a dramatic way of saying that he disappeared from view in the Welsh mist. Elli was to report to him once a year on the affairs of Llancarfan.

When he arrived at Beneventum, he was elected abbot over the large community of monks there, which had just lost its superior. He found that the walls were in ruins, full of gaps, and he got the inhabitants to repair the defences with stone. Not long after, he was made bishop, but did not rule for long. A hostile force attacked the place, broke in, plundering and killing; and a soldier entering the church, transfixed Cadoc with a spear.

For a while the body of the murdered bishop remained at Beneventum, and a church was built over it; but a taboo was placed on all Britons, who were not suffered to enter the town. This was eventually relaxed, and the monks of Llancarfan were allowed to carry off the body. But even at Llancarfan it was not safe. A certain Eilaf, heading a marauding band, drove the monks from their monastery, and as they fled with the founder's body, an irreverent pagan struck the shrine with his staff; whereupon, from within, Cadoc "roared like a bull."

The location of this Beneventum is not certain. It was probably not the Beneventum in Southern Italy. A reasonable guess is that the name is a Latinization of a British name, Ban meaning hill or mountain, and Gwent meaning open country, and not just the part of Wales called by that name. Possibly Cadoc went back to end his days where he had begun under his master Bachan, at the old Romano-British town of Y Gaer or Caer Fenni, supposed to be the ancient Bannium, near modern Brecon. Place names near the Roman site include a hill called I Fenny, a wood called Coed Fenni, and a farm called Fenni Fach, all having the 'ven' of Beneventum. One difficulty with this location is that Britons were prevented from entering the town after Cadoc's death. Perhaps this was an Irish Goidelic settlement, at a time when the Britons were trying to expel the Irish, and this would explain the taboo on Britons there.

St. Canna.

Canna was the daughter of Tewdwr Mawr or Tewdwr Llydaw, son of Emyr Llydaw. She first married St. Sadwrn, her kinsman, who by her became the father of St. Crallo. They accompanied St. Cadfan when he brought a body of British settlers back from Brittany to Britain. After the death of Sadwrn, she married Alltu Redegog, and had by him St. Elian Geimiad, the friend of St. Cybi. She was the mother also by him of St. Tegfan. She is supposed to have founded Llangan in Glamorganshire where so many of the family of Emyr settled, as well as Llangan in Carmarthenshire.

At the Carmarthenshire Llangan (part of which parish is in Pembrokeshire) there is a rude stone which is known as St. Canna's Chair, situated not far from Ffynon Ganna, the saint's holy well. The

St. Canna's Chair.

St. Canna.
From a 15th. century tomb at Beaumaris.

inscription on it is supposed to read CANNA, but its genuineness is doubtful. Miraculous cures were said to have been effected here, especially in the case of persons suffering from ague and intestinal complaints. The patient was required to throw some pins into the well, drink a fixed amount of the water, and sometimes to bathe in it. Then he or she was to sit in the chair for a fixed length of time, and sleep if possible. The process was continued for some days, even for a fortnight or longer. The well dissapeared around 1840. It was said that the hollow in the stone had been produced by the multitude of devotees.

The statue, believed to be of St. Canna, at Beaumaris, shows her holding a staff that seems miraculously to have sprouted leaves.

St. Cybi, Abbot.

There are two Latin lives of this saint. Both are apparently translations from the same Welsh original.

Solomon or Selyf, the father of St. Cybi, was 'princeps militae,' or chief military officer commanding the British. He was also a Cornish king. The title would be equivalent to 'Dux Bellorum' or war-chief given to Arthur by Nennius. Cybi's mother was Gwen, sister of Non, the mother of St. David. He was, accordingly, first cousin to that great saint.

At the age of seven Cybi went to school, and lived thenceforth till he was twenty-seven years old in Cornwall. Then he went on pilgrimage to Jerusalem.

On his return to Cornwall, Cybi probably made his two important foundations of Duloe and Tregony. Duloe is remarkable as having adjoining it Morval, a foundation of his mother St. Gwen, and Pelynt, one of his aunt St. Non. If, as we may suspect, Lansalos (Lan Selyf) was a foundation of St. Selyf, then his father's church was also near by.

Tregony was formerly an important place, on a tidal estuary, and a port, but the river has now been silted up. Adjoining it is Grampound, where again his aunt Non has a church, and as a remarkable coincidence, an inscribed stone, built into the tower at S. Cuby's Church, bears the name of Nonita.

How long Cybi remained in Cornwall we do not know. The 'life' informs us that the natives desired to elevate him to the throne, but that he refused the offer. We may conjecture that Selyf his father was dead, and had been succeeded in turn by Cado, and then by the Constantine whom

Gildas assailed in his tract of 540. Perhaps the Cornish made Cybi the head of an unsuccessful revolt. This would explain why he left his native land for Wales. He took ten disciples with him, four of whom are named, Maelog, Llibio, Peulan, and Cyngar.

Cyngar was in fact his uncle, the founder of Congresbury, which he had abandoned, probably on account of invasions by pirates in the Bristol channel. He was now an old man.

On leaving Cornwall, Cybi went to Morganwg, in which, previously, Cyngar had founded the monastery of Llandough, by Cardiff. Now Cybi was not too well received by king Edelig, but at last the king gave him two sites for churches, Llangibby and Landauer Guir, both on the Usk, in Edeligion (south-west Monmouthshire).

Cybi does not seem to have stayed in Morganwg for long. He went to St. David's, where he spent three days before crossing to Ireland. Then he made his way to the island of Aran Mor, where lived Enda, whom he had previously met on his travels abroad.

Enda had obtained a grant of the island from the king of Munster. Cybi still had disciples with him, and they stayed in Aran for four years. The old uncle of Cybi, Cyngar, was so decrepit that he could not eat solid food, and Cybi bought a cow to supply him with milk.

Maelog, another disciple, cultivated a patch of land near the cell of a priest named Fintan. This led to angry scenes, as Fintan considered this to be an encroachment. St. Enda was called in to arbitrate, but the grievance rankled in Fintan's mind. Cybi's cow had a calf, and it managed to get into Fintan's meadow. The priest impounded it and tied it to a shrub, but it managed to break free and escape of its own accord. Then Maelog

St. Cybi.
From painting on rood-loft,
Lew Trenchard, Devon.

dug up the ground close to the door of Fintan's cell.

Fintan was furious, and betook himself to prayer. He called on God to drive or blot Cybi out of the island. An angel was sent to Cybi to advise him to go. It was clear that the quarrel was going to grow from bad to worse as long as these two saints were near each other. Before leaving the island, Cybi called on God to curse Fintan. The words he used were : "May God destroy him out of this island."

Cybi now tried other settlements in Ireland, first at Meath, where he fasted forty days and nights so as to secure a site as a foundation for himself for ever. But the angry Fintan found him and drove him away. Then he tried Magh-Bregh but within seven days Fintan had stirred up the local people against him. Then he went to Vobvun or Uobiun, but Fintan drove him out after a fortnight. Cybi's patience was exhausted, but before leaving he again cursed Fintan: "May all thy churches be deserted, and may never be found three churches singing at thy altar in all Ireland."

Cybi sailed for Wales, probably landing first at Lleyn, before going on to Anglesey.

He founded a church at a spot called Cyndaf, probably now Llangibi, near Pwllheli, in Lleyn. One day he sent his disciple Caffo to fetch some fire. The oft-repeated story follows, and the disciple returns unharmed with the fire in his garment.

One day, Maelgwn, king of Gwynedd, was hunting when a goat he pursued fled to the saint for refuge. The king demanded the beast, but Cybi entreated that he might be given as much land as the hound could run the goat round. "And St. Cybi let loose the goat, and the hound pursued it through all the promontory, and it returned again to St. Cybi's casula (dress)."

Later, there was trouble between Maelgwn and Cybi, perhaps because his disciple Caffo was the brother of Gildas who had grossly insulted him in his book. The manuscripts of the lives are fragmentary at this point, but it seems that Cybi was obliged to ask Caffo to leave, and that Caffo was murdered soon after. Perhaps Cybi then demanded blood money of Maelgwn. Whatever the truth, Cybi obtained from Maelgwn a fortress at the tip of Anglesey, which thenceforth bore the name of Caer Gybi (Holyhead in English). There the saint settled with his monastic family.

There is a tradition in Anglesey that St. Cybi and St. Seiriol used to meet frequently at midday at the wells of Clorach, in the parish of Llandyfrydog, about midway between Holyhead and Penmon. Cybi journeying from west to east in the morning, and from east to west in the afternoon, had the sun always in his face, and so became tanned; whilst Seiriol who went always with his back to the sun, kept his fair complexion. On that account they are popularly called Seiriol Wyn (the Fair) and Cybi Felyn (the Tawny). The two wells Ffynon Gybi and Ffynon Seiriol were situated one each side of the road leading from Llanerchymedd. Ffynon Gybi was filled up about 1840, when a new bridge was erected. They were formerly much resorted to for various cures.

St. Cybi died on November 8th, certainly after 547, the date of Maelgwn's decease in the yellow plague.

A late mediaeval poem describes Cybi as one of the saints of Brefi's Synod. If true, he probably founded the church of Llangybi, to the south-west of Llandewi Brefi, at that time.

St. David (Dewi), Abbot, Bishop, Patron of Wales.

The most important life of Dewi Sant or St. David was written some 500 years after his death by Ricemarchus (Rhygyfarch), Bishop of Menevia, from 1088 - 1096. There are other Latin 'lives,' but they all seem to be based on this one; there is also a life in Welsh, written by an anchorite of Llandewi Brefi in 1346. Dewi is still the one purely Welsh Saint that has been formally enrolled in the Calendars of the Western Church. It is supposed that his canonization took place in the time of Calixtus II, 1119 - 1124, following on the compilation of his life by Rhygyfarch. It was then that the cult of Dewi, from being that of a local saint, became that of the Patron of Wales.

In writing the life, Rhygyfarch had to rely on oral tradition. The city and church of St. David's had been sacked repeatedly between 795 and 1088. On the last occasion, in 1088, the Cathedral had been completely destroyed, so that few, if any, written documents could have survived.

The name of David's father is given as Sant in Welsh, implying 'a saint' or 'a monk.' He was of the Brythonic family of Cunedda. His mother's name of Non implies 'a nun.' She probably had Irish Goidelic blood in her veins.

Sant was probably a monk in the monastery of Maucen or Mancen at Ty Gwyn on the side of Carn Llidi. This establishment was probably a double monastery, or rather a school to which were admitted pupils of both sexes. Non may therefore have been a pupil when she conceived, and not a nun who had taken vows.

She left the monastery of Maucan and went to a cottage on the cliffs beyond Bryn y Garn, above a little bay which now bears her name. Here she

St. David.
From statue at St. Yvi, near Quimper.

remained till she brought forth her child. There was a certain man in the district, accounted a tyrant by Rhygyfarch, and Non had fled to this place to hide from him. The 'tyrant' was probably Cynyr, her father, who may not have relished the scandal in his family. Later on, Sant and Non came to be recognized as saints themselves, and this enabled the conception to be presented in a different light. Rhygyfarch was able to include a story to the effect that Sant, whilst hunting near the "Old Church" about three miles east of Newcastle Emlyn, was informed by an angel that a virtuous son would be born to him, even though he had embraced the monastic life.

When Non had given birth, Bishop Ailbe, who had refused to say mass with her in the church, came over and baptized the child in a spring at Porth Clais.

David was sent at a suitable age to be instructed at Yr Henllwyn or Vetus Rubus, "the Old Bush," the same place as Ty Gwyn, over which Paulinus was now abbot. The name Alba, or rather Alba Domus, is the Latin rendering of Ty Gwyn or "White Church."

On the slope of Carn Lidi, above Porth Mawr stood "the Old Bush," probably of thorns, where the stone monastery was erected. It probably got the name of Alba Domus or Ty Gwyn when it was whitewashed. It is said to have been founded by St. Patrick.

"And David grew up full of grace and lovely to be looked at. And he learned there the rudiments - the psalms, the lessons of the whole year, and the Mass; and there his fellow disciples saw a dove with a golden beak teaching him and singing the hymns of God."

David remained under Paulinus for ten years. Then it would seem that Paulinus retired, to be

St. Non's Chapel, St. Davids.
Above, remains of masonry;
below, ancient inscribed stone.

replaced by David whose inheritance gave him a right to the post. About the year 527, Gildas appeared on the scene, and, seeing David as the head of the community whilst still quite young, he tried to oust him and take on the government himself, probably to turn it into a daughter house to his great settlement in Armorica. When Cadoc refused to become involved, Finnian of Clonard was called in to arbitrate, and he pronounced in favour of Dewi, no doubt because of his family.

But David did leave the monastery for a while, having placed his uncle Guistlianus in charge. Whether it was at this time, or some other that he established some of his many churches in South Wales, we do not know. It seems likely that he established churches in Gower after the expulsion of the Goidels. It is also probable that at some period, he travelled through Dumnonia to Cornwall and thence to Brittany, where his principal foundation is at St. Divy, near Landernau in Leon. Perhaps he went there during the outbreak of the yellow plage which raged in Britain from 547 to 550, as did St. Teilo. The story that he went to Jerusalem is possibly a mediaeval invention aimed at establishing the independence of the Welsh Church from the see of Canterbury.

But wherever he travelled on that occasion, when he returned to the Old Bush, he found his uncle Guistlianus still there. David had come to the conclusion that the site was undesirable. He said to him: "From this place scarce one in a hundred will go to the Kingdom of God. I know another spot whence few will go to hell; for every one who shall be buried in that cemetry in sound faith will obtain mercy." David's motives for the above were no doubt of a practical nature; at any day a pirate vessel might land there, destroy the monastery, and easily cut off all escape in the direction of the mainland. It was expedient for them to go further inland, and to settle on a spot concealed from the sea, and less exposed.

The old site was now given up, and David and his disciples Aidan, Teilo and Ismael, with others unnamed, migrated to the new locality. This was Glyn Rhosyn, in the valley of the Hodnant.

They settled there in the evening, and lit a fire. Now nearby, at Clegyr Fwya (the Rock of Boia), lived an Irish freebooter who had settled there and who terrorized the neighbourhood.

In the morning he saw the smoke of David's fire, and his wife goaded him to drive them out. Boia went, but David easily pacified him. Boia's wife, however, was highly incensed when she heard that the settlers were monks from "the Old Bush" and she resolved to be rid of them.

Accordingly she sent her maids to bathe in the stream close to where the saints were. Some of the monks complained to David that this would become unendurable if repeated daily. But he assured them that the girls would soon tire of their bathing if they took no notice of them.

As Boia refused to molest the monks, his wife resolved to propitiate the underground divinities with a sacrifice. She invited her step-daughter named Dunawd to pick nuts with her one warm day, and, when she had persuaded the girl to rest her head in her lap, she shore off her hair and cut her throat, pouring the innocent blood to the gods.

This did not produce a result, and the woman ran away, afraid of her husband's wrath when he knew she had killed his daughter. The following night, an Irish pirate ship landed. The pirates found the entrance to Boia's fort ungarded, burst in and slew Boia in his bed.

David was now able to proceed with the construction of his monastery. It was probably of stone, as no timber of any size grows in those parts. David devoted himself wholly to prayer, study, and the training of his disciples. But life in the monastery was not always a bed of roses. On one occasion David's steward attempted to murder Aidan, his favourite disciple. On another occasion a visiting Irish saint with a fiery temper killed the boy whom David had assigned to wait upon him, with a single blow of his fist. The penitential code of David shows that much wild blood was to be found in his and other monastic settlements of the period. Severe penalties had to be adjudged in cases of drunkenness, murder and attempted murder, and other gross crimes. Kissing a girl had to be expiated by three days' penance. It would seem that David's rule was seen as too strict to please all the monks, for on one occasion his steward, cook and his deacon tried to poison him. But St. Scuthin who was on a visit from Ireland, suspected something, and announced that on that day he alone was going to wait on David. Then the deacon, fearing that the plot was discovered, turned pale and retreated in confusion. The bread that had been offered to David was thrown away, and a dog that ate some of it died almost at once; also a crow. An investigation was held. "And all the bretheren arose and lamented, and cursed those deceitful persons, the steward, the cook, and the deacon, and with one voice damned them and their posterity, that they should forfeit their place in the kingdom of heaven for ever."

Except when compelled by necessity, David kept aloof from all temporal concerns. He did not attend the Synod of Llandewi Brefi when convened by Dyfrig. As no agreement could be arrived at there relative to matters in dispute, Paulinus advised that he should be sent for, and Dyfrig and Deiniol went to fetch him. On his arrival he advised them to move from the old Roman station of Loventium to a mound at Llandewi Brefi, where speakers could stand and be heard. It would seem that this Synod was called together in order to enact canons of discipline; the story that it was primarily to deal with the Pelagian heresy is possibly an addition by the mediaeval biographers.

David's activities, and perhaps also those of his fellow monks, are witnessed by churches bearing the name of Dewi in Herefordshire, in Monmouth, Brecknock, and Radnor, as well as in Ceredigion and Pedydiog, and Gower and the lands between the Tawe and the Towy. There are also dedications to him in S. W. England and Brittany, and he is credited with having provided Ireland with a form of the Mass.

At length David's strength began to fail. He said Mass and preached to the people one Sunday, and on the following Tuesday, being March 1st., he was in the Church, as he had continually been for several days, and early in the morning he listened to his monks singing the psalms. Then falling into ecstasy he exclaimed: "Raise me after Thee," and expired. At the very moment of his death his old companion St. Kentigern, had a vision whilst praying at Llanelwy; he saw him enter heaven, conducted "with heavenly music into the joy of the Lord, crowned with glory and honour."

The year of his death was possibly 589.

St. Deiniol, Abbot, Bishop.

Deiniol or Daniel was the son of Abbot Dunawd Fwr, son of Pabo Post Prydyn. He is often called Deiniol Wyn, the Blessed. He was the brother of Sts. Cynwyl and Gwarthan, and the father of St. Deiniolen. His grandmother was Dwywai, daughter of Lleenog.

Pabo and his family, having lost their territories in North Britain, retired to Wales, where they were well received by Cyngen, king of Powys, who granted them lands, and whose son and successor Brochwel married Arddun, Pabo's daughter. His son Dunawd, embracing the religious life, founded the monastery of Bangor in Maelor, otherwise Bangor Iscoed, on the Dee, with the assistance of Cyngen, and later of Brochwel, who generously provided for it. It seems likely that Dunawd's three sons helped him in the foundation of his monastery, but Deiniol does not seem to have remained there long. He left Powys for Gwynedd, where he founded the monastery of Bangor in Carnarvonshire, under the patronage of Maelgwn Gwynedd, who largely endowed it with lands and priviliges, and, it is said, raised it to the rank of an episcopal see. Here Deiniol spent the remainder of his days as bishop.

We know little of the early years of Bangor in Arfon, or Bangor Fawr, as compared with other Welsh monastic foundations. Some of the sons of Helig ab Glannog were monks in it; and on the destruction of Bangor Iscoed by Ethelfrid in 607 or 613 some of the monks that esacaped came hither. Deiniol is said to have been succeeded by his son Deiniol the Younger; and the next bishop whose name is known was Elfod, styled Archbishop of Gwynedd, who died in 809.

Deiniol was present at the Synod of Brefi.

St. Deiniol.
From 15th. century glass,
Llandyrnog Church, Denbighshier.

St. Dubricius (Dyfrig).

The oldest life of St. Dubricius is found in the Book of Llan Dav written in the twelfth century. Unfortunately much of the life and particulars of land grants in that book have been modified to suit its aim of reclaiming properties which once belonged to the saint but which were then in the diocese of Hereford. There is, however, some information about St. Dubricius in the 'Life of St. Samson' which was written much earlier by a monk of the monastery of Dol, in Brittany.

The story of Dubricius begins in what is now Herefordshire, in the small Celtic kingdom of Erging or Ercych. Pepiau, the king, had been away on a military expedition. On his return he found that his daughter was in the family-way. He was angry and ordered her to be put in a skin bag and thrown into the river. She was, however, washed ashore, so he sentenced her to be burnt alive, but when the king's messengers went to inspect the ashes, they found her sitting on the pyre nursing her new-born son. Pepiau ordered them to be brought to him, and when he let the child stroke his cheeks he found that it cured him of a drivelling mouth, a long-standing ailment. Pepiau then granted to the child the place where it had been born, which was called Matle. The place is now called Madley. It is about seven miles from Hereford, and a Roman road passes through it in the direction of Abergavenny.

We have no reliable information about the early life of Dubricius, nor his instruction. The first monastic settlement made by him was at Henllan, now Hentland on the Wye, about four and a half miles north-west of Ross. He must have been one of the most important saints and teachers of his times for it is said that he gathered as many

St. Dubricius.
From ancient roll, copied in one of the Dugdale mss., in the Bodleian Library.

as two thousand disciples there.

He remained at Henllan for seven years, and then he began a new settlement at Mochros, now Moccas, about five miles from Madley. He seems to have founded other settlements in the Golden Valley, at Cum Barruc and perhaps also Abbey Dore. In fact, he and his disciples may have set up as many as two dozen establishments in what is now Herefordshire.

It was the custom of the early Celtic saints to seek a retreat in lent, away from their teaching and other duties. For this purpose he seems to have founded the abbey on Caldey Island near Tenby. He also received a grant of Penally on the mainland exactly opposite Caldey. Perhaps this was given him in recognition of his founding the abbey on Caldey. Penally is known as the birthplace of St. Teilo; it is also famous for its ornamented Celtic stone cross. Whether Dubricius had any contact with the young Teilo is not certain, but it is by no means impossible.

Dubricius is also said to have had a foundation in Gower, and the dedication of the parish church of Porlock in Somerset (in documents of the 15th. and 16th. centuries) implies that he or his monks were involved in the great missionary expansion which went out from South Wales.

Dubricius lived and died somewhere between the years 450 and 550. He died on Bardsey Island on November 14th.

Some years after the saint's death, in 577, the battle of Deorham took place. This led to settlements of the Hwiccas on the lower Severn, and no doubt to raids over the Wye into the kingdom of Erging. The monasteries of Dubricius and his disciples in Ewyas and Erging were utterly wasted, and the monks escaped carrying their relics and books with them. "Be it known," says a charter of the time, "that great tribulations and devastations took place... due to the heathen Saxon race, and it was mainly on the confines of Britain and Anglia [towards Hereford], and it was so extensive that the whole borderland of Britain was almost destroyed... and mainly about the river Wye, on account of wars and frequent daily and nightly incursions, on one side and on the other. After a while, peace having been established, the land was restored by force and vigour (to its rightful owners); but it was swept bare and unoccupied, with men few and far between."

We know that some of the monks of Dubricius took refuge with St. Teilo at Llandaff. Later on, the Church of Llandaff took over the abandoned sites of Dubricius' foundations. Thenceforth the Church of Llandaff assumed itself the legitimate inheritor of all the possessions of Dubricius. It had harboured the refugees; it had kept their Books of the Gospels with their marginal records of grants of land. This explains why the compiler of the Book of Llan Dav aimed at recovering possessions of Dubricius from the see of Hereford; but Dubricius had probably never really had anything to do with Llandaff, which may not even have been founded until after his death.

BARDSEY ISLAND.

St. Ernin.

According to the Myvyrian Archiology, Ernin was the son of Helig ab Glanog, of the race of Cunedda, whose territory was overwhelmed by the sea. It is partly covered today by the Lavan Sands, between Carnarvonshire and Anglesey, and it extended to the Great Orme's Head. Some of Helig's many sons, Ernin among them, on losing their patrimony became saints or monks in Bardsey.

He may be assumed to be the St. Hernin known in Brittany, and there is a version of his life contained in the book by Albert the Great. According to this, Hernin was a native of Britain in the sixth century, who crossed over into Armorica, and settled as a hermit in Duault, near Carhaix, on land given to him by a British chief who had established himself there. He lived there until his death, which occurred on the first Monday in May. He was buried in his hermitage and a great stone was placed over his grave.

One day, Conmore, Count of Poher, before he became regent of Dumnonia, was hunting nearby, when the stag he was pursuing fled to the saint's oratory, and laid itself down on his tomb, where the hounds did not venture to attack it. Struck by this marvel, Conmore made inquiries, and then ordered a chapel to be erected over the grave. When the workmen came to begin the chapel, they found that the birds had collected twigs and leaves and had heaped them up, forming a little green bee-hive hut over the tomb.

A number of saints bearing the name Ernin occur in the Irish Martyrologies.

St Ernin.
From statue at St. Nicholas, Prisiac.

St. Eugrad.
From a statue at Treouergat.

St. Eugrad.

Eugrad or Eigrad was son of Caw, and brother of Gildas. In the 'life' of the latter by the monk of Ruys he is called Egreas. He says: "Egreas, with his brother Alleccus (Gallgo) and their sister Peteova (Peithian), a virgin consecrated to God, having given up their patrimony and renounced worldly pomp, retired to the remotest part of that country (Anglesey), and at no great distance from each other, built, each one for himself, an oratory, placing their sister in the middle one. Both of them alternately, each on his own day, used to celebrate with her the Daily Hours and the Mass, and taking food with her after Vespers, and returning thanks to God, they returned before sunset, each to his own oratory... They were buried in the oratories which they had built, and are preserved there, famous and illustrious for their constant miracles."

Eugrad is also said to have been a member of the congregation of St. Illtyd at Llantwit. There is an Ergyryat, who may be the same person, in the story of 'Culhwch and Olwen;' he is described as having been at one time a knight in the service of king Arthur.

He was one of the family of Caw who received a grant of land from Maelgwn in Anglesey. The oratory or church he founded is Llaneugrad, which adjoins the settlement of his brother at Llanallgo.

St. Gildas.

Gildas is best known to us as a writer of books. Some of what we know comes from what he has to say about himself in his book 'De Excidio Britanniae.' There is also a 'life' written originally in the ninth century by a monk of Rhuys in Brittany.

Gildas was born in Arecluta (the country "on the Clyde") and was the son of Caw. This was the year of the victory of Ambrosius, about 476.

The Picts and Scots eventually obliged the sons of Caw to seek refuge in Wales, where they were granted lands in Anglesey by Cadwallon Lawhir, probably around the year 506. Only one of the brothers of Gildas stayed behind. His name was Huail, and he lived a wild piratical life.

Gildas is said to have had five children: Cenydd, Gwynog, Nwython, Maidoc or Aidan, and Dolgan. Assuming these children were not just spiritual, then perhaps he lost his wife whilst in Anglesey, and resolved on the religious life. For his training he placed himself under Illtyd at Llantwit, where he was in the company of Samson, Paulinus, and David. Whilst he was at Llantwit, Illtyd seems to have been busy reclaiming fertile land by placing a sea wall along the banks of the severn.

The life written at Rhuys adds that Gildas also studied at other schools besides that of Illtyd. He seems to have gone to Ireland at the end of this period, and there he met St. Brigid.

Whilst Gildas was in Ireland, his brother Huail had become such a nuisance to his own race that they held a council of war, and slew him. Welsh traditional sources imply that it was Arthur who killed Huail. Gildas returned to Britain to demand blood money of Arthur, and the story says that Arthur surrendered several parcels of land to the family of Caw.

About this time the Battle of Badon took place, and soon after, around 520, Gildas went to Rome. On his way back he landed at Rhuys in Brittany, and obtained a grant of land there. During this period, St. Brendan paid him a visit, possibly in the winter of 523-4. Gildas wanted Brendan to stay and look after his new foundation, so that he might be free to go to Britain in search of new disciples for his monastery. But Brendan refused the offer. Gildas, however, returned to Britain after having spent seven years abroad: "At the end of the seventh year he returned, with a large mass of volumes, to Greater Britain... and great numbers of scholars flocked to him from all parts." His austere practice is shown in the following extract from his life: "It was his habit to go into a river at midnight, where he would remain unmoved until he had said the Lord's prayer thrice. Having done this, he would repair to his oratory, and pray there on his knees unto the Divine Majesty until broad daylight. He was wont to sleep moderately, and to lie upon a stone, dressed only in a single garment. He used to eat without satisfying his wants, contented with his share of the heavenly reward."

During his time in Britain, he looked after the monastery at Llancarfan, whilst St. Cadoc went away for a year. We have already told the story of Gildas and Cadoc spending lent on the islands in the Bristol Channel.

The ravages of pirates caused Gildas to move to Glastonbury, where he was well received. "He built a church there... in which he fasted and prayed assiduously, clad in goats' hair, giving to all an irreproachable example of a good religious life."

At length, after seven years' absence, Gildas

St. Gwynog, son of Gildas.
From stained glass at Llanwnog.

returned with a body of recruits to Rhuys, and the monastery was organized on an extensive scale.

It was some ten years after his return to Rhuys that he wrote 'De Excidio Britanniae,' or the Ruin of Britain.

When quite old, he was summoned to Ireland by king Ainmire, who wanted him to help restore the religion there. This was in 565. David was also invited, but there is no indication that he went there personally. It appears that he sent some trained monks in his stead. Ainmore asked Gildas to stay in Ireland. He declined to do so, but "he went about all the territories of the Hibernians, and restored the churches, instructed the whole body of the clergy in the Catholic Faith, that they might worship the Holy Trinity... and drove away from them heretical conceits with their authors." This is the exaggeration of an author of a 'life' written several centuries later. No doubt Gildas did something; he built monasteries and furnished the churches with a form of Mass such as was said at Rhuys; but he was too old to do more.

He returned to Armorica, feeling that his end was approaching, and he left the monastery of Rhuys to die in peace in the island of Houat. His last request was that his body might be placed in a boat and committed to the waves. It perhaps shows a lingering in his mind of the pagan idea of shipping the dead to the Isles of the Blessed beneath the setting sun.

His wish was complied with, but local people, in their greed for relics, pursued it in boats. However, before they could reach the drifting coracle a wave upset it, and the body sank.

Gildas died on January 29th., probably in the year 570, and his age was given as 94.

St. Gildas.
From 15th. cent. statue at Locmine.

St. Germanus,
Statue at Pleyben.

St. Illtyd.

St. Illtyd appears to have been one of the most important teachers of his time.

He was a native of Armorica, but of British stock. He was educated in "the seven sciences" by St. Germanus. But he had no desire to embrace the monastic life, and he crossed the sea and served under King Arthur, who was said to be his cousin. He was married and Trynihid, his wife, was a virtuous woman.

After a while, he left Arthur and attached himself to Paulinus or Paul of Penychen, a cantref in Mid-Glamorgan.

It would seem that his conversion dates from this period, from a time when he nearly lost his life in a swamp.

Illtyd then withdrew from the service of Paul of Penychen, and went, "accompanied by his wife and attendants," to the banks of the Dawon in South Glamorgan, "and it being summer time, he constructed a covering of reeds, that it might not rain upon their beds; and while their horses were depastured in the meadows, they slept the night away, their eyes being heavy."

During the night, Illtyd had a dream which confirmed his resolution, and he made up his mind to leave his wife.

In the morning, he roused his wife and told her to go and see to the horses. When she returned, naked and shivering, instead of allowing her into the bed, Illtyd threw her clothing to her, and told her to dress and be gone. The poor woman wept, but Illtyd was resolute in his purpose. He dressed himself and set out for Hodnant, a pleasant dip among low hills, watered by a tiny stream. Having made up his mind to settle there, he went to St. Dubricius where he was shaved and received the monastic habit. Then he returned to Hodnant and Dubricius marked out for him the bounds of a burial place, and in the midst of this, Illtyd built a church of stone and surrounded the whole with a quadrangular ditch. Here he lived an ascetic life, bathing every morning in cold water, and rising to prayers in the middle of the night.

Hodnant, now Llantwit, was an attractive site near the Severn Sea.

One day, Meirchion, king of Glamorgan, was hunting, when a fawn he was pursuing fled for refuge to Illtyd's cell. When the king saw the beast crouching at Illtyd's feet, he did not venture to kill it. He ate a meal of broiled fish provided by Illtyd. This food was not to his liking, but he slept the night there, and awoke the following morning in a better temper, confirmed Illtyd in his holding of the Hodnant valley, and granted that he should make of it a tribal school. Illtyd kept the fawn with him and tamed it to draw wood and do other light domestic tasks.

This incident took place early, when Illtyd had few disciples. Once he had the security of tenure, disciples flowed to him from every quarter, among them men of good family. "He had labouring men to till the soil. Seed multiplied, and toil met with abundant reward." As scholars he had Samson, Paul, and David. He seems also to have taught Gildas, and possibly Maelgwn Gwynedd.

Meanwhile, Illtyd's wife had herself been leading a devout and virtuous life, but an irresistible urge to see her husband came over her. She found him working in the fields, but he refused to listen to her and denied her hospitality. They never met again.

Illtyd had trouble with two of king Meirchion's stewards who seem to have begrudged his holdin land without paying tax. Illtyd found the an-

St. Illtyd.
Statue at Locildut, Sizun.

noyance of these men so intolerable that twice he retreated to a cave by the river Ewenny, leaving Samson in charge of the monastery.

On the death of the second steward, who fell into a swamp, Illtyd returned to Llantwit, and remained there unmolested.

Hearing of a famine in Armorica, he ordered vessels to be laiden with grain, and, along with these ships, he sailed to Brittany. The natives there specially needed seed-corn, which he was able to provide. Their gratitude was great, and they urged him to stay in his native land, but he returned to Glamorgan. In his old age, he is said to have returned again to Brittany, and to have died there at Dol. But there is uncertainty about where he died, whether in Brittany or Wales. He died on November 6th., probably between the years 527 and 537.

The memory of Iltyd is honoured in Wales on account of his having introduced an improved method of ploughing. A Welsh Triad says that he was one of the "three knights of the Court of Arthur who kept the Holy Grail," the other two being St. Cadoc and Peredur.

About four miles from Brecon, there is a well-known cromlech called 'Ty Illtyd' (Illtyd's house) so-called because of a popular idea that the saint had made it his hermitage.

Ty Illtyd.

St. Mabenna.
Stained glass, St. Neot.

St. Mabenna, Virgin, Abbess.

This saint was one of the many daughters or grand-daughters of Brychan, who settled in north-east Cornwall when expelled from Brecknockshire. She is not named in the Welsh lists, but is given in Leland's 'Itinery' and by William of Worcester.

The only church dedicated to her is St. Mabyn, on a wind-swept hill, but with pleasant wooded vales in the folds of the upland country. The church tower is fine and serves as a landmark.

Without doubt, this saint did not plant herself on this bleak hillside, but made her cell in one of the combes that dip to the Alan or the Camel, probably at Treveglos (Tref-Eglwys), where there is a holy well, a quarter of a mile north of the village.

Nicholas Roscarrock, who gives as her day Nov. 18th., says: "There used to be a hymn sung of her, signifying she had twenty brothers and sisters, whereof Sts. Endelient and Miniver were two."

St. Mabenna is represented crowned, and bearing a palm in one hand and a book in the other, in the Wives Window at St. Neot.

St. Padarn.

Padarn's parents seem to have come from Brittany to Wales, possibly fleeing from one of the dynastic revolutions that took place there.

According to the legend, which is late, dating from the eleventh century, Padarn was trained for the religious life in Ireland. When his education was complete he returned to Britain with the puropse of returning if possible to Armorica. Among his disciples were three who were said to be his cousins, Hetinlau, Catman, and Titechon (or Tinlatu, Cathinam, and Techo as they stand in the St. Malo Breviary). In Cardigan he founded the great monastery of Llanbadarn, near Aberystwyth. It was for a while an episcopal see, before becoming absorbed in that of St. David's. It is said that he ruled at Llanbadarn for twenty-one years. At the end of this time he departed. The legend states that he became Bishop of Vannes in Brittany, but it is not certain that he can so be identified with Paternus of Vannes. There are, however, two parishes dedicated to St. Padarn in a district called Petherwin, on the Cornish side of the Tamar, but just in Devon. Perhaps this is where he went from Wales.

St. Sidwell.
From a statue in St. Sidwell's Church, Exeter.

St. Paul or Paulinus.

The Life of St. Paul of Leon by Wormonoc was written in 884. The author stated that he had based his work upon an earlier 'life,' and that what he had added was oratorical flourish.

Paulinus was born in Penychen (in what is now south-east Glamorgan) about the year 480. He had eight brothers, of whom two only are named, Notolius and Potolius, and three sisters who are numbered amongst the saints. One of his sisters was called by Wormonoc Sitovolia, whom we may identify with St. Sativola or Sidwell of Exeter. From the legend of another sister, Jutwara, we ascertain the that the third of the holy sisters was Wulvella. These names have been Anglicized and Latinized almost past recognition in their original form.

Wormonoc tells us that the family lived in a district called Brehant Dincat which Doble has identified as Llandovery in Carmarthenshire, for it was in the parish of Llandingad (which contains the name of Dincat).

Against his father's wishes, Paulinus was at an early age sent to St. Illtyd at Lantwit, and was placed by him at Ynys Pyr or Caldey Isle. Whilst under Illtyd, he made the acquaintance of Sts. David, Samson, and Gildas. He and they were afterwards moved to Llantwit where they were probably employed by Illtyd in banking the Severn so as to reclaim tracts of rich alluvial soil; they also had the task of scaring away the birds.

At the age of sixteen, Paulinus seems to have become bored by the work of dyke-making and bird-scaring, and he and twelve other rebels went away and set up wattled cells and built an oratory near the limits of his father's land. Wormonoc says that Paulinus lived for some years there in great sanctity, drinking only water, eating nothing but fish and vegetables, and clothing himself in skins. He was ordained priest during this period, perhaps by Dubricius.

The sites of Paulinus' foundations during this period are discussed by Doble: They include what is now the village of Llanddeusant, a few miles from Llandovery, which may have been within the family estate, and which may have taken its name of Llan of two saints from Paulinus' two brothers, Notolius and Potolius. Another site could have been at Llangorse, near Brecon, which has been described in old documents as a Paulinus church, and near which there is a "well of the twelve saints" which could refer to the twelve who left Llantwit with Paulinus.

Rhigyfarch introduces Paulinus twice into his 'Life of St. David.'

Eventually Paulinus went with his companions to the court of King Mark Conomanus, who ruled at "Caer Banhed" over four tribes "speaking four languages." This Mark appears to be the king of Cornwall made famous by the Arthurian legend of Tristan and Isoude. The reference to four tribes seems to have been copied from Bede's account of king Oswald!

King Mark had seven bells, with which he summoned his nobles to dinner. Paulinus coveted one of them, and asked for it. The king refused, and the saint left him in a huff. These Celtic saints thought that they had taken over from the bards, whose prerogatives included a right to demand things without being refused. The 'life' says that Paulinus then visited his sister, and that later he crossed to Brittany.

Paul landed first with a group of disciples on the island of Ouessant. There he built a monastery

St. Paul of Leon.
From statue at Lampaul-Guimiliau.

Group of crosses at Ploudalmezou.

consisting of a chapel and thirteen little huts of stone and turf. His name is preserved there in the port of Porz-Pol, and the village on the site of his monastery, called Lampol. Then Paulinus sailed to the mainland of Brittany. One of his first settlements now bears the name of Lampaul Ploudalmezou, where there were many megalithic remains. He and his followers sanctified some of the menhirs that had religious cults, by incising them with crosses.

Next, Paulinus went east, to Roscoff, and thence to the isle of Batz, where he met Withur, his cousin from Gwent, who was well-established as a noble there.

Withur gave the island of Batz to Paulinus, and there is a legend that he delivered the island of a monstrous serpent or dragon... In order to safeguard his new establishments in Brittany, Paulinus went to Paris, to Childebert, king of the Franks, who consecrated him bishop. Paul had also established a principal monastic centre in the ruined town of Ocsimor, and from there he went out with great energy to convert his diocese. This foundation, in an old ruined town, grew into the fine city of S. Pol-de-Leon.

During his time at Batz, he was visited by St. Brendan, perhaps in 526. In his old age, Paulinus retired twice, but his retirements may have been politically motivated, during a period of troubles when Judual was attempting to overthrow the usurper Conmore. According to his biographer, he was 100 years old when he died.

The year of his death was possibly 579.

Paul or Paulinus was also known as Pol in Brittany, and Paulinus Aurelianus in Britain.

The fame of the British Paulinus has been overshadowed by an English saint of the same name, Paulinus of York, whom we know from Bede.

St. Rumon or Ruan.

This saint seems to have been known as Roman or Rumon in Devon, Ruan in Cornwall, and Ronan in Brittany.

He is probably the Ronan who was consecrated bishop by St. Patrick, and who is said to have visited Scotland.

He made a foundation at Romansleigh, originally Lan Roman, in Devon. From there, he seems to have moved west into Cornwall.

A parish near Porthleven still bears his name as St. Ruan Major. Another of his foundations is Ruan Lanihorne. The name Lanihorne itself is a corruption of Llan-ruan. There is a holy well in the village there. At the mouth of the Fowey he founded a church called Llan-ruan, corrupted in Domesday to Lanlaron; but the port or basin of the harbour still bears his name unaltered as Polruan.

From Cornwall he crossed to Brittany. There he eventually planted his hermitage on a height on the flanks of the Menez Hom, near Quimper. The local people were made up of the ancient non-Aryan race and British immirgants who had assumed the lordship over them. The natives were pagans. Ronan worked hard to convert the heathen, and thereby provoked some hostility. In particular, a woman named Keban opposed him, perhaps because her husband had been converted and she was afraid of him being turned into a monk. Keban accused Ronan of being a werewolf, and she laid this charge before Gradlo the British king. Gradlo solved a difficult situation by suggesting that Ronan be presented to his wolf dogs, who would surely attack him if he were a wolf. In the event, the two dogs came and licked Ronan's feet.

St. Petroc, Abbot.

According to the life of St. Petroc by John of Tynemouth, he was the son of Glywys, king of Glwysing. His eldest brother was Gwynllyw the warrior. He left South Wales "rejecting the vanities and transient allurements of the world; despising worldly for heavenly things, he began to adhere firmly to God, and gave up his country, his kindred, and at last all the things of this world. Leaving home, he reached Cornwall, in the district called Botomeni (Bodmin), where, throughout his life, he served God most devoutly, and erected a very large monastery in his honour."

The Welsh pedigrees, however, say that he was a son of Clement of Cornwall; but the two may be reconciled perhaps on the basis of one of them being his spiritual father. We may also note that there were many settlers from Wales in north-east Cornwall, perhaps including this Clement.

Petroc is said to have entered a monastery at an early age. After some years, he went over to Ireland where he studied for twenty years. Then he returned to Cornwall, accompanied by his disciples, and landed at Padstow. It seems that St. Samson was staying there at that time. St. Petroc visited him, but was given a somewhat cool reception; but it was Samson who left, and Petroc stayed in Padstow for about thirty years.

He was wont daily to to stand from cock-crow to dawn in the water chanting psalms. He ate nothing but bread, except on Sundays, when he had a good bowl of porridge.

The 'life' then takes on a mythological nature. Petroc went first to Rome, then Jerusalem, and then India, where he fell asleep on the beach. On awaking, he saw a large silver bowl moving towards him across the waves. It was large, so

St. Petroc.
From the rood screen,
Lew Trenchard, Devon.

he planted his staff and set down his sheepskin, and climbed into the silver vessel. At once it took him over the waves to a certain island where he landed. He spent seven years there, living all the while on a single fish which he caught daily, but which always returned sound to be eaten again.

At the end of seven years, the shining bowl reappeared and returned him to his beach in India. He found his staff and sheepskin where he had left them, guarded by a wolf. Then he returned to Cornwall, and the tame wolf went with him.

This legend is no doubt derived from a pagan myth of a divinity sailing in a silver bowl of the moon over the heavenly ocean.

When he reached Cornwall he found that the people there had forgotten that he had once predicted the weather wrong for them. Back in Padstow he eventually obtained grants of land from Tewdrig, a notorious tyrant, and later from Constantine. He is, in fact, said to have converted Constantine. One day when he was hunting a fawn, it sought refuge under the saint's coat. Petroc was thus enabled to found his great monastery at Bodmin. The spot he chose was occupied by Guron, a hermit, who surrendered it to him.

Petroc died at an advanced age on June 4th.

The year of his death was around 590.

Petroc's body remained at Bodmin until 1177, in which year it was secretly carried off to the Abbey of St. Mevin in Brittany. The prior of Bodmin went to king Henry to complain about the theft, and the king sent letters commanding Roland de Dinan, Justiciary of Brittany, without delay, to cause the body to be restored. Which it was, "and the sacred body was restored in all its integrity, without the least diminution; the abbot and monks of St. Mevin having sworn on the relics belonging to their church that they had not retained any portion of the body."

St. Samson presiding at the Council of Prelates.
From 13th. cent. window, Dol Cathedral.

St. Samson.

Samson's father was Amwn, of Demetia (but perhaps descended from Emyr Llydaw), and his mother was Anna, daughter of Meurig ab Tewdrig, a king of Morganwg.

When quite young he was sent to St. Illtyd to be educated. He studied hard, and his master was said to be the most learned of all the Britons in the Scriptures, in Philosophy, to wit, Geometry, Grammar, and Arithmetic.

At the age of fifteen Samson began to practise fasting, but was reprimanded by St. Illtyd, who said, "My little son, it is not proper that you should injure the health of your small body in its early bloom by excessive abstinence."

Illtyd employed his pupils in repairing the old dykes that had been erected by the Roman legionaries to keep out the tides of the Severn.

On a Sunday, when Dubricius visited the monastery for the purpose of conferring orders, three were submitted to him, two to be ordained priests, Samson to be received into the diaconate. Then it was, as the three knelt, that a dove flew in at the window, and when the bishop raised his hand to lay it on the candidate for the diaconate, the bird perched on Samson's shoulder.

The favour shown to Samson by his master roused the jealousy of two of the bretheren, nephews of Illtyd. What they dreaded was Samson aspiring to the succession after Illtyd, for he was first cousin to him. These two brothers resolved on getting rid of him.

They prepared a poisoned herbal drink for him, but did not succeed in killing him.

Samson was ordained priest, and again the dove appeared, but visible only to Dubricius, Illtyd, and Samson himself.

Samson began to feel uneasy at Llantwit because of the prejudice against him, but he said nothing. One day, however, Illtyd himself recommended that he should go to the monastery at Ynys Pyr or Caldey Isle, which was presided over by "an illustrious and holy priest" named Pirus.

In his new quarters, Samson became more strict than before in his mode of life. No one saw him idle; he was continually occupied reading, writing, or in prayer, when not engaged on the manual tasks imposed on him.

Whilst Samson was at Ynys Pyr his father fell ill and it was feared he might die. The old man sent for his son. Samson's reply to his father's messengers was, "I have left Egypt, why should I return thither?" But Pirus intervened and made him go.

Samson selected a young deacon as companion, and they set out with two horses. They passed through a dense wood, and the strange sounds, the hooting of owls, and cries of hawks filled the deacon with terror. Then they heard a human voice hallooing. The deacon panicked, let go of the bridle of the horse he was leading, threw away his cloak, and fled. A woman issued from the shade, grey-headed, with wildly-flowing hair, and carrying a boar-spear in her hand. Seeing the young man running she threw the spear at him, but without hitting him; however, he fell in a faint on the ground.

Samson tried to rouse him, and then called to the old woman. She came hesitatingly, not wishing to lose her spear. "You hideous creature! Who and what are you?" rudely inquired the saint.

The poor woman said she belonged to the original inhabitants of the land, but that she, her mother and eight sisters were all that remained. Her husband was dead. Samson told her to revive the deacon, but she said she could not, whereupon he cursed her to die on the spot. Then she fell down to the left, and expired.

On reaching his father's house, Amwn ordered everyone outside, except his wife, son, and the deacon, and before them he confessed the sins of his past life. Then, urged by Anna his wife, he vowed to dedicate himself to God, and insisted on having his hair clipped immediately. Not content with this, Anna said they should devote all their offspring, and surrender their possessions. Amwn agreed, and Samson accepted five of his brothers, but he refused the one sister as he saw that she would be addicted to the vanities of the world.

At the same time Umbrafel and Afrella, his uncle and aunt, asked to enter the religious life. Samson made arrangements for his mother and aunt, and asked his father and uncle to accompany him to Ynys Pyr.

Amwn and Umbrafel divided all that they possessed into three portions, one for the Church, one for the poor, and the third they reserved for themselves. Their sons and daughter got nothing.

When Samson arrived at Ynys Pyr, he found that Dubricius was there for lent. Apparently the story of the death of the woman in the forest had got about, and Dubricius felt he should investigate it. He summoned the deacon and tried to get the truth out of him. That Samson had killed the poor creature could not be denied; the question was whether he had knocked her on the head, or had merely killed her with his curse. She had belonged to one of the aboriginal native tribes, and these people were credited with being given over to necromancy. The woman, on her own confession, was a witch, or so the deacon said, and it was a command of Moses, "Thou shalt not suffer a witch to live." Seeing that there was no other witness, Dubricius accepted the deacon's version.

Dubricius now appointed Samson as steward of his monastery. This upset Pirus; he complained that Samson had been wasteful with the honey (or mead!), but Dubricius looked into this and decided that the charge was unfounded. It seems that Pirus was replaced because he had taken to drink. Soon after, one night, this "eminent man and holy priest" got drunk and fell into the well. The monks heard him howl, and quickly pulled him out, but he died the same night.

Samson began to reform the monastery, which led to tension between himself and his monks. About eighteen months later, some Irish monks returing from Rome visited the island, and Samson took the opportunity to go to Ireland with them, leaving his father and uncle behind. He stayed there for some time, founding churches at Ballygriffin, in the county of Dublin, and Bally Samson in South Wexford.

He returned to Ynys Pyr, and, finding that his uncle had made some progress in religion, he sent him to Ireland to a monastery that had been committed to him. He refused to take over the running of the monastery at Ynys Pyr, and went with four companions, including his father, to an isolated creek at Stackpole. There he settled his companions in an ancient camp, and himself in a cave where he could spend most of his time alone.

After a time, Dubricius, acting in concert with a synod, sent him a letter requesting his presence. He could not refuse, and Samson ended up at the head of the foundation at Llantwit, at a time when St. Illtyd had to go into retreat because of the vexations of the king's stewards.

One night, it was revealed to him that he was to quit Britain, and go to the land that had been so extensively colonised from that island. This happened when Illtyd was able to resume as abbot, and Samson was required to step down. Samson therefore resolved to go to Armorica.

He seems first to have sailed around the Severn estuary, and thence to Cornwall where he landed at Padstow. There he made a little foundation where is now the site of his chapel and cemetery. He left his boat, loading his possessions on to a chariot he had brought back with him from Ireland. He seems to have had the idea of crossing over to southern Cornwall, to take a ship from the south coast for Brittany. It appears that he spent some considerable time there, as is witnessed by his having made other foundations, one at Southill, near Callington, and another at Golant. His disciples also made settlements there, as St. Mewan and St. Austell.

During his travels in Cornwall, Samson came across a group of people dancing around a standing stone on the hill of Tregeare. He remonstrated to them, but the people explained to him that no harm was meant; they were merry-making as was their immemorial custom; but some advised him to mind his own business. Samson, however, persisted in his denunciation of the ceremony, and, after a boy had been thrown from a colt, and revived by Samson, they listened to him. But instead of destroying the stone, he cut a cross upon it. The revellers gave up their dancing for that year, to resume it the next anniversary.

Eventually, he crossed with his disciples over to Armorica, landing at Guioult. The land there was low and marshy, except for Mont Dol, which must have attracted them, but had been already occupied, perhaps as a fortress. One day, in the vicinity, Samson came across some locusts settled on some brambles. "Ha," he exclaimed, "Locusta

- in this locus sta! We will accept this as a command and here abode." This was the beginning of Samsons famous foundation at Dol.

When Samson arrived there, the usurper Conmore was acting as regent for Childebert, king of the Franks. Conmore had treated many of the saints badly, and Samson saw an advantage in replacing Conmore by the rightful heir, Prince Judual. Now Judual was held in honourable captivity in Paris, so Samson went there to ask Childebert to release him. At first Childebert resisted, but, afraid of Samson's anger, he eventually let him take the prince back to Brittany with him. Judual began a rebellion, and Conmore marched against him and was defeated in two battles; in a third he was killed by the young prince himself, on the slopes of the Monts d'Arrée.

The success of the revolution meant that Samson and the other abbots who had helped, were now in favoured positions. Samson went in his Irish chariot back to Paris, to obtain confirmation from Childebert of various land grants that had ben made to him. On his return, he made Dol his permanent residence. He was said to have been 120 years old when he died, but this may be an exaggeration; it was on July 28th, possibly in 565.

St. Samson sailing towards Armorica.
From 13th. cent. window, Dol Cathedral.

St. Seiriol.

Seiriol was said to be the son of Owain Danwin, and brother or nephew of Einion, prince of Lleyn, in Carnarvon, of the race of Cunedda. Einion established a sacred tribe at Penmon in Anglesey, and made Seiriol chief of the saintly tribe. So celebrated did this establishment become under him, that foreigners, even vikings, are said to have resorted to it for instruction. Seiriol and Cybi were friends, and we have already explained how they came to be called the Fair and the Tawny.

Late in life, Seiriol retired to Glanach (Priestholm), a little island off the coast. This islet is now called Ynys Seiriol. He lived in the early part of the sixth century.

St. Seiriol.
15th. century glass at Penmon.

St. Teilo.
From 15th. Century glass at Plogonnec, Finistere.

St. Teilo.

Teilo is one of the most important of the Welsh saints. His 'life' is contained in the Book of Llan Dav or Liber Landaviensis. This book was drawn up in the twelfth century for the purpose of establishing the rights of Llandaff against those claimed by the see of St. David's and the see of Hereford. It cannot therefore be trusted as a reliable account of history. Doble has pointed out that the older St. Chad Gospels do not suffer from this drawback, and that they contain marginal entries which mention the 'Altar of Teliau,' the 'familia Teliavi' or monks of Teilo, governed by the 'Bishop of Teiliau.' Although claims have been made that Teilo was the founder, and first bishop of Llandaff, it is now believed that his monastery referred to in the Book of Chad was in fact at Llandeilo Fawr, or Great Llandeilo. The link with Llandaff was that eventually all the properties of Llandeilo Fawr were transferred there.

Teilo was born at Penally, near Tenby, and opposite Caldy Island. Whether he ever had any contact with, or teaching from St. Dubricius will probably never be established. It is more certain that he was instructed by Paulinus, at Ty Gwyn, where he met St. David as a fellow pupil. When David started his independent foundation in Glyn Rhosyn, where now stands the cathedral that bears his name, Teilo went with him.

The 'life' says that David, Teilo and Padarn went on pilgrimage to Jerusalem. This may be true, but there are those who think it was invented by Welsh sees in Norman times to resist encroachment by Canterbury.

Apart from his principal monastery at Llandeilo Fawr, Teilo obtained grants of land, and founded a large number of monasteries and churches. But in 547 appeared the yellow plague againt which there were no known medicines. Teilo resolved to flee along with his community. He took with him a large number of bishops, and a great many men and women, and escaped into Cornwall, where he was well received by king Geraint. Then he sailed across to Armorica and visited St. Samson at Dol. He stayed in Armorica for seven years and seven months, and he left a number of foundations there, many retaining his name.

When Teilo died it was at Llandeilo Fawr in Carmarthenshire. It is said of him when asked by St. Cadoc, "what is the greatest wisdom in a man" that he replied, "to refrain from injuring another when he has power to do so." He is celebrated in the Welsh Triads as one of the three "Blessed visitors of the Isle of Britain," the other two being Sts. David and Padarn.

St. Tudwal, Bishop.

Tudwal who is described by the Welsh as Saint and Bishop, is known in Brittany as Tugdual or Tual. All that can be said of Tudwal's origin is that he was a native of Britain, and his mother's name was Pompaea. Our front cover shows the two of them leaving Britain in a ship bound for Brittany. It is said, in fact, that they travelled there along with seventy-two monks and servants.

These immigrants landed at the south-west point of Leon, where Tudwal established his 'lan' beside one of the little rivers that discharge into the port of Conquet. This bore the title of Lan Pabu, as Tudwal being abbot went familiarly by the title of father. At that time all Leon was under the rule of Deroch the second king of Domnonia. Deroch confirmed the possession of Lan Pabu to Tudwal; but he did not stay there long. As soon as he had organized his establishment, he went on a tour of the whole of Domnonia, planting other centres whence his monks might disperse. Then he went on to Treguier, where he founded a large monastery called Val Trechor. He went to Paris in order to have his foundations ratified also by the Frankish king Childbert I, and, having obtained this and become a bishop, he went back to Treguier, where he remained till his death. He is said to have died on November 30th., 553.

St. Tyssilio (Suliau)

Tyssilio or Suliau was the son of Brochwel of Powys. His mother was Arddun, daughter of Pabo Post-Prydain. He had two brothers, one of whom was Cynan Garwyn. He was first cousin to St. Asaph and St. Deiniol.

His father Brochwel was reigning prince of Old Powys, and resided at Pengwern or Shrewsbury, where Tyssilio was probably born. From an early age, Tyssilio resolved on embracing the religious life, but his father, self-willed and headstrong, destined him for the profession of arms. Thus, one day, Tyssilio took flight whilst out hunting, after having announced his resolve to his brothers.

He went to Meifod, and threw himself at the feet of Abbot Gwyddfarch. Brochwel sent some men to Meifod, with orders to bring him back; but as he, already a monk, steadfastly refused, they did not use force and break sanctuary, but returned and reported the situation to Brochwel.

Brochwel allowed him to go his own way, but Tyssilio was afraid he might one day use force, and he asked to be allowed to go to a more remote spot, and he was sent to Inis Suliau, an islet on the Menai Straits, where he founded the church of Llandyssilio. He spent seven years there, and then returned to Meifod.

Some time after, Gwyddfarch the abbot died, and Tyssilio succeeded him.

Now a terrible thing happened to the British. Ethelfred of Northumbria came west. He crushed the British kingdom of Elmet on his way, and at Chester he fought against Brochwel.

For the battle, hundreds of monks had assembled on a hill above the field, to pray for victory, and perhaps also to curse the enemy. Many of them were butchered, and Brochwel, who was old by

St. Tyssilio.
From statue at S. Suliac.

then, escaped with some of his men. The result of this battle was that the British in what is now Wales became permanently cut off from those in the northern kingdom of Strathclyde. The battle of Deorham, fought in 577, had previously cut off the British in the south-west penninsula.

Brochwel died, and his son who succeeded him died two years later without issue. His widow, a strong-minded woman, resolved on withdrawing Tyssilio from Meifod, marrying him, and making him king of Powys. But Tyssilio hated war, and above all, objected to marrying his brother's widow and giving up the religous life. His sister-in-law, like a woman, took this as a personal offence, and began to do everything she could to annoy the monks of Meifod, including seizing the abbey's revenues. To free his monks from persecution, Tyssilio fled, along with a few of his monks who were attached to him, crossed the sea to Brittany where he sailed up the estuary of the Rance, and landed by a little creek. There he resolved on settling. He built a chapel and some cabins for his brother monks, and tilled the soil. Slowly, his monastery grew from its modest beginnings. He received news that his sister-in-law was dead and an invitation to return to Wales, but he was content to stay where he was. Some time after that he died in his monastery, but in what year we do not know; it was possibly around 650.

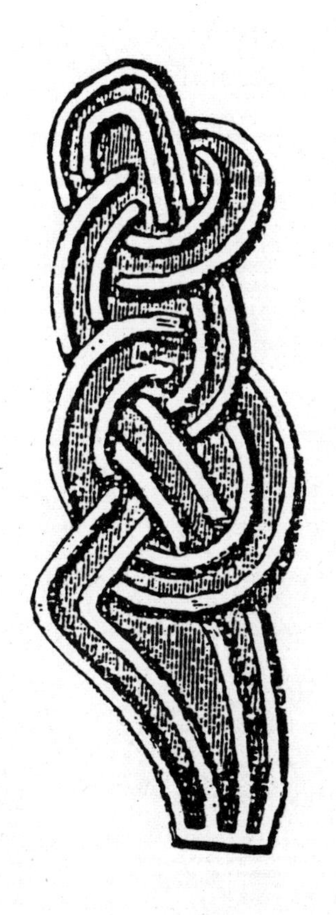

Design on ancient stone,
Llandevaelog, Brecon, Wales.